CONCEPTS IN COMPUTING

Kenneth Hoganson
Kennesaw State University

JONES AND BARTLETT PUBLISHERS
Sudbury, Massachusetts
BOSTON   TORONTO   LONDON   SINGAPORE

World Headquarters
Jones and Bartlett Publishers
40 Tall Pine Drive
Sudbury, MA 01776
978-443-5000
info@jbpub.com
www.jbpub.com

Jones and Bartlett Publishers
Canada
6339 Ormindale Way
Mississauga, Ontario L5V 1J2
CANADA

Jones and Bartlett Publishers
International
Barb House, Barb Mews
London W6 7PA
UK

Jones and Bartlett's books and products are available through most bookstores and online booksellers. To contact Jones and Bartlett Publishers directly, call 800-832-0034, fax 978-443-8000, or visit our website, www.jbpub.com.

Substantial discounts on bulk quantities of Jones and Bartlett's publications are available to corporations, professional associations, and other qualified organizations. For details and specific discount information, contact the special sales department at Jones and Bartlett via the above contact information or send an email to specialsales@jbpub.com.

Production Credits
Acquisitions Editor: Tim Anderson
Production Director: Amy Rose
Associate Production Editor: Mike Boblitt
Production Assistant: Sarah Bayle
Editorial Assistant: Melissa Elmore
Senior Marketing Manager: Andrea DeFronzo
Manufacturing Buyer: Therese Connell
Composition: Northeast Compositors, Inc.
Cover Design: Kristin E. Ohlin
Photo Research Manager: Kimberly Potvin
Cover Image: © Natthawat Wongrat/ShutterStock, Inc.
Printing and Binding: Malloy, Inc.
Cover Printing: Malloy, Inc.

Library of Congress Cataloging-in-Publication Data
Hoganson, Kenneth.
  Concepts in computing / Kenneth Hoganson.
    p. cm.
  Includes index.
  ISBN-13: 978-0-7637-4295-9
  ISBN-10: 0-7637-4295-3
  1. Electronic data processing. I. Title.
  QA76.H5863 2007
  004—dc22
                              2007011607

6048

Printed in the United States of America
11 10 09 08 07   10 9 8 7 6 5 4 3 2 1

Dedicated to my wife, Mary, for all her patience and encouragement.

Preface

Concepts in Computing provides an introduction to and an overview of computer science, including an introduction to the theoretical, engineering, and applied knowledge domains that compose the discipline. The text provides an overview and introduction to concepts and fundamental "key ideas" and innovations of computer science.

GOALS

One of the purposes behind the development of this textbook is the need to facilitate the success of students entering into the study of computer science. A second synergistic goal is to generate excitement, curiosity, and enthusiasm for learning more about the science of computing. The philosophy underlying the approach of this textbook rests on the idea that the brilliant and fascinating key concepts in computing are inherently so interesting and enticing that a clear and clean introduction to these key concepts themselves will generate intellectual excitement in the student and the desire to learn more.

A third goal of the textbook is to provide a solid grounding in the science and engineering of computing for interdisciplinary students and students focusing on the social science and business aspects of computing. This single textbook provides that foundation in a way that can be covered in a single semester course so that students are not required to take separate courses in computer architecture, data structures, networking, security, and the like.

This frees up an interdisciplinary curriculum or information systems curriculum to focus coursework in other targeted areas.

While building a level of interest and excitement, the text also provides a solid foundation for further in-depth study in any area of computer science while making important connections between the subdisciplines within computer science. Students learn faster and integrate knowledge more efficiently if they can see how each subject area connects with, and is interdependent upon, other areas.

TEXTBOOK PHILOSOPHY

This introductory survey textbook requires only a modest understanding of mathematics and saves many formal presentations for later study. Knowledge of digital computer electronics or digital logic is not required as a prerequisite. Specific chapters will address these knowledge areas and fill in the basics in each area. The prerequisite knowledge needed for each chapter is given in the chapter introduction.

The idea that more students would study computer science when first enticed with easy and exciting applications before switching to more rigorous fundamentals has been tried with many different strategies: from introducing Web page design to game programming or whatever the latest "hot" technology is that students hear about. In general, this approach has been less than satisfactory, because students must first learn the fundamentals of the science over multiple terms to get to the exciting applications, particularly in the case of game design. Students who find the key concepts in computing uninteresting—something to simply "wade through" to get to the "exciting" part of computing—will be more interested in applied computer science or information systems.

Many strategies have been attempted to increase retention and student success in their first computing courses: teaching with simple robots, teaching with software robots, teaching using pseudocode only, teaching with visual programming, teaching with AI-logic languages, teaching assembly/machine code, teaching object-oriented programming, teaching using Web page design, teaching with game design, teaching with UML and analysis and design, and teaching with simplified languages. All of these attempts are intended either to generate greater student excitement or to simplify the introduction to computer science and logical problem solving. Each method had some success with the instructor who came up with the technique—which unfortunately has not been universally translatable, with the possible exception of teaching a first programming course with a language specifically designed as a teaching language (i.e. BASIC, Pascal, Alice). The conclusion: There is no "magic bullet" that will make computing and programming easy while attracting new students and increasing enrollment.

In contrast, this text takes a direct approach by introducing students to the key concepts in computing so that students will understand what computer science is about and see how the various knowledge areas support each other. This approach also provides an answer to the pesky question that is on the tip of many a student's tongue: Why must I first learn foundation material?

A program-of-study that begins with and is centered on programming without an overview of the discipline may inadvertently discourage some students who desire more than a career in programming. This broad-based introduction to computing can precede the student's first programming experience, may be conducted in parallel with the first programming experience, or may follow the student's first programming course.

A side benefit of this direct approach is that students will be able to evaluate whether computer science is their "cup of tea" much sooner. Students will be much better served with the information needed to make this decision early, rather than later and only after investing multiple semesters or years of effort. We owe it to our students to give them an understanding of what they can look forward to.

The best way to introduce students to computer science, which is an inherently complex field, is with a clear presentation designed to make complex topics easier to understand. This text follows this approach, introducing complex topics in a straightforward way, so that:

1. The learning curve is no higher than it absolutely has to be.
2. Students get a sense of the wide variety of computing areas and disciplines and a taste of the interesting problems areas that await exploration. (Computer science is not *just* programming!)
3. Those students who like analytical problem solving will see their future success in this field.
4. Students begin to see the connections between the different areas of computer science, allowing them to see for themselves the answer to the question "Why do we have to learn this?"

Students coming to computing from disparate foundations, generally lack an overall appreciation of what computer science is, how it evolved from older disciplines, and how it is spawning new disciplines and connections with other fields. All students entering into the study of computer science are already familiar with the machines and are experts in using them for many tasks, both significant and mundane. Students are often exposed to computers in preschool, yet typically do not understand what the machines are really all about. Students new to computing generally cannot make informed decisions about whether they would like to invest their education in the computing discipline.

ORGANIZATION

The order in which the chapters are included in the book ensures that the student will have the prerequisite knowledge needed to absorb the content of each subsequent chapter, but other orders are possible within the prerequisite knowledge constraints of Figure P.1. This figure shows prerequisite knowledge dependencies as arrows that connect chapters. A chapter with an arrow leading to a subsequent chapter contains prerequisite knowledge that is needed as a foundation for the subsequent chapter.

Figure P.1 also illustrates the division of the text into four sections:

- Foundation Concepts
- Software and Programming Concepts
- Computer Systems Concepts
- Advanced Concepts and Applications

Software/programming/design and **computer systems/computer architecture** are the backbone of the textbook and are critical to understanding computer science. These two themes are, of course, interdependent and come together in Chapter 14 on parallel computation, which is an area that is both hardware and software intensive. Chapter 14 is a low-intensity introduction to this advanced knowledge domain.

A third important theme in computer science is the **theoretical foundations** of the discipline. This text includes an introduction to theoretical foundations but does not attempt to provide a thorough overview of this area. The text includes a substantial introduction to theoretical topics through various chapters:

- Chapter 7, Complexity and Algorithm Analysis
- Chapter 12, Models of Computation
- Chapter 13, Artificial Intelligence
- Chapter 14, Parallel Computation
- Appendix B, Boolean algebra

This textbook can be applied in a variety of different settings that include:

- **CS0: A first course in computer science for majors.** This text *does not* focus on the ordinary computer user–type applications, but instead

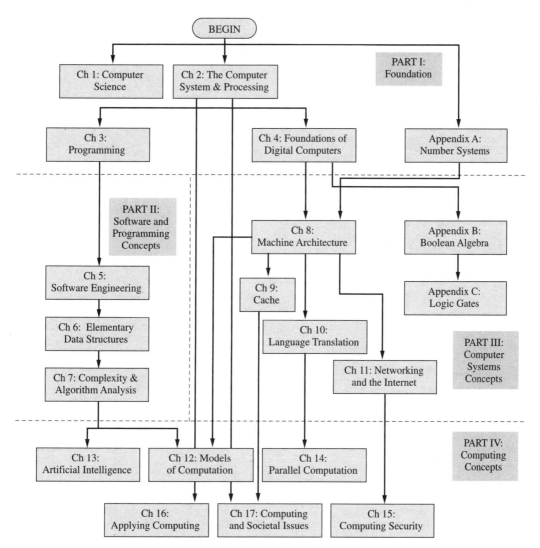

FIGURE P.I Chapter Linkages and Prerequisite Knowledge

conducts a survey of the science and engineering of the discipline as its introduction. Instructors can supplement the theoretical and hardware foundations content in this textbook with the application areas of their choice: Web page design, database, or beginning programming.

The content is presented at a basic level with the emphasis on clarity, so that it requires nothing more than basic mathematics (algebra) as a prerequisite and does not require a prerequisite in programming.

TABLE P.1   Suggested Chapter Coverage and Sequence

Chapter	CS-0	CS-1&2	Graduate	Inter-Disciplinary	IS/MIS
Ch 1: Computer Science	1	1	1	1	1
Ch 2: The Computer System	2	2	2	2	2
Ch 3: Programming	3	3	3	3	3
Ch 4: Digital Computers	4	4	4	4	5
Ch 5: Software Engineering	5	5	5	7	6
Ch 6: Elem. Data Structures		6	6		7
Ch 7: Complexity & Analysis		7	7		8
Ch 8: Machine Architecture	7		11	9	9
Ch 9: Cache			12		10
Ch 10: Language Translation	8		13	10	11
Ch 11: Networking & Internet	9		14	11	12
Ch 12: Models of Computation			15		13
Ch 13: Artificial Intelligence			16	12	14
Ch 14: Parallel Computation			17	13	15
Ch 15: Computing Security	10		18		16
Ch 16: Applying Computing	11	9	19	5	17
Ch 17: Societal Issues	12	10	20	6	18
App. A: Number Systems	6	8	8	8	4
App. B: Boolean Algebra	O		9		
App. C: Logic Gates	O		10		

Table P.1 provides a suggested chapter sequence for this text used as the primary CS0 course textbook.

- **CS1–CS2: First programming sequence for computer science majors.** This text will work as a supplement to a textbook on programming in a specific language. Adding this text as a supplement broadens the CS1–CS2 sequence so it becomes more than just an introduction to programming in the language of choice; it also becomes an introduction to computer science as a discipline. The supplement concept is particularly useful for computing programs that do not have a dedicated CS0 course as a prerequisite, but instead launch directly into CS1 and programming in depth.

Many introductory programming textbooks can provide only the briefest of introductions, with limited breadth of coverage of computer science and the variety of theoretical and applied topics. This text allows the instructor to assign chapters and sections for outside reading while lectures focus on learning programming. The interested and advanced students can whet their appetite for more knowledge by reading ahead; extra credit readings and assignments from the supplement can be included to add variety, breadth, and additional learning to a course without impairing the primary focus on programming. The introduction to the concepts of data structures (Chapter 6) and object orientation can enhance the students' learning in that critical area. Students generally find the use of a second source and reference when studying to be very helpful, particularly when studying difficult topics like data structures. When using this text to supplement the programming sequence, the introduction to the various areas of computer science can be spread across both courses at an easy pace that allows most of the students' attention to be concentrated on the programming learning objectives of the course sequence.

- **Graduate Introduction to Computer Science:** Many computer science graduate programs have a course, track, or set of courses designed to facilitate the entry of non-CS-degreed students into computer science. Students come from a variety of undergraduate disciplines: information systems, computer engineering, software engineering, information technology, mathematics, physics, electrical engineering, and so forth. These students are generally knowledgeable about computers and have experience using them but lack the breadth and depth of an undergraduate degree in computer science. This textbook remedies that situation and builds a stronger foundation for graduate computer science study. This textbook could be required in a seminar series, introductory course, research methods course, directed study, or even used as a self-study. It has proven itself in this setting at the author's home institution and has even been requested by students who have undergraduate CS degrees but have been out of school for a while and need a review of the discipline. In this role, the textbook fills in many gaps and makes connections in the students' knowledge about the discipline, while strengthening the students' base of knowledge for further study.

- **Interdisciplinary and Multidisciplinary Studies:** As computer science has matured, much of the excitement and dynamism is now being generated "between the cracks" of the traditional disciplines in interdisciplinary studies and research. Biotechnology using supercomputing for gene analysis and bioengineering is an obvious example. This textbook is ideal for introducing students who have a background in any of the physical sciences to the computer science discipline. It is an excellent introduction for students who need to understand computing in order to apply the tools and techniques of computer science to efficiently solve problems in their discipline.

- **Technical Foundation for Social Computing Disciplines:** Information systems (IS) and management of information systems (MIS) students who focus more on the social aspects of applying and managing computing systems and resources in social and business environments need a foundation in the technical side of computing, but not at the same level as the computer science student. IS and MIS students need an understanding of computer architecture, but not an entire CS course in the field. IS and MIS students need an understanding of data structures, but not at the same level as a computer-science student. IS and MIS students need to understand the fundamentals of operating systems, networking, and security, but not with the same degree of technical depth as a computer science student.

   This text can provide the overview of technical computing topics that IS and MIS students need as the context for their work. The use of this textbook in an undergraduate or graduate IS/MIS curriculum has the potential to provide that needed foundation in a single course, freeing up space in the curriculum for other courses. The modest mathematical prerequisite (algebra) makes these technical topics accessible for the nontechnical student without requiring a deep structure of prerequisite knowledge. This freedom also allows for the possibility of sharing a foundational course between the technically oriented and social/business-oriented computing disciplines.

CONCLUSION

Computing programs often begin by delving into a succession of mostly loosely connected areas (or seemingly so to students): perhaps programming first, then perhaps computer organization and architecture, followed by mathematical foundations, and so on. Students are expected to master each knowledge area in great detail and demanding rigor without the benefit of first seeing how each area fits into and contributes to a greater whole. Some students switch from computing after their first courses in programming because they conclude that computer science *is* programming, and they don't want to program for a living or have concerns about the long-term career prospects as a programmer. They can't see the forest because they are forced to first concentrate on what appear to be unrelated trees. By showing them the forest (breadth of computer science) as this text does, students can then make connections between the knowledge areas, realize that there are many different facets to computing and computer science, and also learn that a career in computing will not be a static job in programming, but will evolve as the technology advances and new ways to apply computing technology are discovered.

Because this text is a presentation of the exciting key concepts in computer science with the intention of drawing students into the excitement of discovery and the desire to learn and study more, the text does not provide an in-depth presentation in any single area. The overview presented here will set the foundation for future learning in each area while "whetting the appetite" with the joy of discovery.

SUPPLEMENTS

Instructors using this text in a classroom setting have access to the following support materials at http://www.jbpub.com/catalog/9780763742959/:

- Answers to the Exercises
- PowerPoint slides with illustrations from the text

The following introductory chapters are also available from Jones and Bartlett Publishers:

- José Garrido's *Alice: The Programming Language*
- Richard Schlesinger's *Visual Basic .Net: The Programming Language*
- Bradley Miller and David Ranum's *Computer Science: The Python Programming Language*
- Jules Berman's *Ruby: The Programming Language*
- Jules Berman's *Perl: The Programming Language*

For information regarding bundling options please contact your Jones and Bartlett Publisher's representative at 1-800-832-0034 or visit http://www.jbpub.com/computerscience.

ACKNOWLEDGMENTS

I would like to thank the following reviewers for their valuable input:

Herbert L. Dershem, Hope College
Henry A. Etlinger, Rochester Institute of Technology
Robert Franks, Central College
Raymond Greenlaw, Armstrong Atlantic State University

Terry L. Herman, Bowling Green State University
Chung Lee, California State Polytechnic University
Frank Malinowski, Armstrong Atlantic State University
Peter Sanderson, Otterbein College

Thank you to the supportive staff at Jones and Bartlett Publishers: Tim Anderson, Amy Rose, Mike Boblitt, Kimberly Potvin, and Melissa Elmore.

Contents

CHAPTER 2   The Computer System and Basic Instruction Processing Function   31

CHAPTER 3   Programming   51

PART 4   ADVANCED COMPUTING CONCEPTS   167

CHAPTER 12   Models of Computation   169

CHAPTER 13   Artificial Intelligence   179

CHAPTER 14   Parallel Computation   189

CHAPTER 15   Computing Security   203

CHAPTER 16   Applying Computing   209

CHAPTER 17   Computing and Societal Issues: Ethics, Global Computing, and Academic Integrity   217

APPENDIX A   Computer Number Systems   223

PART ONE

Foundation Concepts

Computer Science

The mind is not a vessel to be filled,
but a fire to be kindled.

—Plutarch

Chapter 1 covers the discipline of computer science, the key concepts underlying both theory and practical engineering, and computer science's relationship with other computing disciplines. In addition, it covers the continued fragmentation of the discipline into offshoot specialized disciplines. **Prerequisite knowledge needed:** None, simply an interest in computing.

1.1   WHAT IS COMPUTER SCIENCE?

Computer science is a scientific and engineering discipline that investigates all aspects of computing with computing machines. Computing is about problem solving and about applying computing technologies to improve human existence. Compared to the natural sciences like physics and biology, computer science is different in that it investigates an artificial, human-created world. In a natural science, the knowledge in the discipline progresses through the familiar "hypothesis and experiment" cycle to acquire and validate new knowledge. In computer science, the discipline advances through proof of theory and demonstration, with experiments used to confirm theory after an appropriate device, software, or technique has been created. Often, computer simulation is used to confirm the value of new ideas, techniques, and theory, particularly when building a prototype for testing that may require millions of dollars. Confirming theory through simulation is a weaker proof than experimenting in the natural world, because the simulation is itself a creation that may contain errors or assumptions and biases of the scientist, while true experiments that test against uncaring nature are truly impartial.

Computer science also shares much with mathematics, because mathematics also studies a world of logic, but it is the logic of numbers. Mathematics investigates concepts that are not explicitly part of the physical world, but are applied in a conceptual universe of thought and the logic of numbers. Perhaps not coincidentally, the rules and laws of mathematics can be used to model the physical world with great effect, assuming that the mathematical model is correctly designed. Put another way, we can model the world and its behavior using mathematics, and the predictions based on mathematics hold true in the "real" and physical world. Computers and software also obey logical rules that are a part of the mathematical universe; that universe is also extremely useful in modeling the "real" world through simulation.

Computer science also shares much in common with the engineering disciplines. Engineering is the a study of how to build and construct useful things in a particular domain. For computer science, the construction domain is computing machines, logic, and programming.

The roots of computer science lie in both mathematics and electronics engineering, both of which spawned offshoot disciplines: computer science growing from mathematics focusing on theoretical concepts and software, and computer engineering diverging from electronics engineering, emphasizing the design and fabrication of computers (Figure 1.1). Another discipline has emerged from computer science called *software engineering*, which attempts to study how to build software with the certainty and predictability of the traditional engineering disciplines. Currently, much of software designing remains more an applied art or craft than engineering, but the goal is to improve the accuracy of the software design process and the

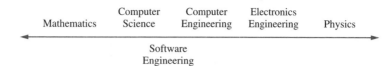

FIGURE 1.1   Computer Science and Related Disciplines

reliability of the resulting software, as well as to reduce the time required to complete a project.

The success of applying computer science, computing systems, and software has spawned a number of interdisciplinary fields:

- Information systems: the application of computing technology to organizations and businesses
- Geographical information systems: the application of computing technology for representing geographical information, used heavily by cities and governmental organizations
- Bioinformatics: the application of computing technology to biological systems; one area is representing genes and DNA
- Biomedical systems: the application of computing technology in medical domains and patient care and histories, for use by medical practitioners
- Information technology: the study of the management and maintenance of computing systems, including networking, operating systems, hardware, and software
- Information security and assurance: an emerging field investigating the vulnerabilities and weaknesses of computing systems (both hardware and software) to threats, and how to insulate and protect systems and reduce their vulnerability

There are various subdisciplines within computer science itself, ranging from mathematically based, to engineering oriented, to applied. There are areas called *graph theory* and *formal languages*, which are very mathematical. These crossover knowledge areas are part of computer science because they have important applications in that discipline and contributed to the theoretical foundation of computer science, but otherwise would reside happily within mathematics. The study of computer architecture and high-performance computing is a subfield within computer science that also exists in, and overlaps with, computer engineering. The study of database theory and systems is an application of computer hardware and software, which exists only because computers exist. Other fields in a constantly expanding list include:

- Computer architecture
- Computer networking

- Formal languages
- Data structures
- Compilers
- Programming languages
- Graphics
- Artificial intelligence
- Database
- Software engineering
- Human–computing interaction
- Data mining
- Game design

The high profile of the high-tech computing fields has diminished somewhat of late, because the science and discipline of computing has matured as part of the natural evolution of a sciences discipline:

1. At first, an emerging discipline is a mere offshoot and sideshow of the mature and established parent discipline (computer science from mathematics).
2. Then as a critical mass of important applications and foundations are discovered, the discipline continues to build followers and excitement. Funding and economic opportunities are ripe.
3. The critical mass of activity reaches full flower, and applications and technologies translate into products that change our everyday lives and reach into and change other disciplines of learning and study.
4. The rate of dramatic change in the discipline begins to diminish because the broad foundations of the science have been discovered, tested, and verified. Further changes tend to involve applications and specialized or splinter disciplines, rather than fundamental theory, but not exclusively. The growth of employment opportunities may slow as the science and technology is integrated into the economy.
5. The maturation process continues. The rush of opportunities and the excitement of dramatic discovery moderates as the discipline evolves toward applications of the science and specialization into new disciplines and subdisciplines. It is important to realize that a new discovery that can shake-up and rejuvenate a discipline may occur at any time.

Today's computer science shows signs of being in stage 4, generating much excitement in emerging and developing interdisciplinary knowledge areas, while at the same time undergoing important advances and improvements in many areas of the discipline. The application of this textbook for interdisciplinary studies that relate computing and other science is timely.

Computer Science?

- Computer science: the study of the **science** of computing
- Computer science: the **engineering** of **applications** and systems involving computing machinery
- Computer science: a study of **complexity** and methods to manage complex systems
- Computer science: the study of **systems** (hardware and software), methods, applications, and approaches to **managing information**
- A diverse mix of all of these.

Computer History Museum

E stablished in its new home in 2002 in Mountain View, California, the museum hosts exhibits on computing hardware and software artifacts including portions of the Zuse Z3 machine, the Atanasoff–Berry machine (John Atanasoff of Iowa State University), and other early computers in addition to the ENIAC. See www.computerhistory.org.

1.2 KEY CONCEPTS IN COMPUTER SCIENCE

A number of key concepts and ideas form the foundation for the modern computing system. The computer and these foundation concepts have evolved over time, through the work of many scientists and engineers. This textbook provides an introduction to computing and computer science by illuminating these key concepts:

The Computer System

The computer system itself contains a number of key ideas:

1. **CPU:** The basic computer requires a central processing unit (CPU) that executes instructions from a program, which is stored in the computer's memory. With the development of the computer, mankind now has its first man-made servant that can autonomously carry out a set of instructions and accomplish many kinds of useful work far faster than a human can. The CPU contains special storage areas called *registers* and

has internal connections to move data within the various parts of the CPU.

2. **Instruction execution cycle:** This key idea originated with early computers and has remained a core concept even in the modern computer that has many performance enhancement features. The basic idea is that the CPU fetches instructions, one at a time, from a program that is stored in the computer's memory, does the commands ordered in that instruction, and then goes back to the program in memory to fetch the next instruction in the list.

3. **Simple computer instructions:** The design of the computer's low-level set of instructions is tightly interwoven with the design of the computer's internal architecture. The description of the set of possible instructions that the computer must perform is a specification for the design of the CPU chip itself.

4. **Architecture layers:** Like many complex systems, the computer is designed as a set of components or pieces assembled together. This compartmentalization design concept also is useful when viewing the computer system as a set of layers, each of which can be examined separately, but integrating with the rest of the system.

5. **Operating system:** The operating system is a system of software components, rather than hardware, that is responsible for making the hardware useful by managing the resources of the computer system and providing the user interface. As a set of software components, the operating system can be revised, configured, and updated as technology evolves. In this way, a computer system can evolve and keep up with technological advances over its lifespan, even though the hardware itself is "frozen" as a physical device that cannot be modified, only replaced.

Programming

Programming is the art of writing software instructions to control the computer. This skill takes time and effort to develop. It is central to understanding computer science and other computing disciplines, but is less important for other related disciplines such as information systems. This text includes an overview of some programming concepts, but is not intended to teach programming.

Software Development Cycle

It has been observed that programmers repeat a design cycle of just a few steps when programmers build software, repeated multiple times. The programmer analyzes a portion of the task, designs a solution and strategy for this piece of the problem, codes it in a programming language, and then tests the project and design constructed so far. Any detected problems are fixed, and the designer moves to the next task and the cycle repeats.

Complexity and Algorithm Analysis

Analyzing and exploring the behavior of programs and their efficiency is an important aspect of computer science. The performance of algorithms is important in planning the amount of computing power needed as the size of the data grows. Some algorithms perform well with small amounts of data, but perform poorly with large data sets. Software designers and programmers must understand the performance of their algorithms in order to anticipate whether the computer will be able to complete the required work in the expected time frame.

Software Engineering

Software engineering is the study of the process of designing software and writing programs. The goal is to make the process more reliable and efficient.

Boolean Algebra

Computers are logic-processing machines, and their function and behavior can be represented and modeled logically and mathematically. Boolean algebra is an extremely simple algebra that is used to model how computers work at a very low level, manipulating binary digits that have only two states: 0 and 1. This low-level engineering of the computer is easy to understand. The complexity in computers is built by combining many layers and pieces of logic into a complex whole. As you begin to understand how the computer functions at a low level, you begin to pierce the mystery of how the computer does what it does. Knowing that the machine is inherently simple and logical clearly indicates that the machine will behave in consistently predictable ways, thus the machine can be understood and mastered by anyone. An introduction to this topic is contained in Chapter 4, and additional optional material follows in Appendix C.

Logic Gates from Transistors

The Boolean logic of the computer must be implemented in hardware at a low level. In the modern computer, very efficient microscopically tiny transistors are used to build logic building blocks called *gates*. Only a few transistors are needed to implement the logical operations needed, and then these logic constructs (the gates) are used as building blocks to build more complex functions, and ultimately the computer system itself.

CPU Design

The internal design of the central processing unit is fascinating for a couple of reasons. The internal design of the CPU reflects the design of the machine language to the point where the computer's low-level machine language is almost a specification for the design of the CPU itself. The second fascinating area is exploring the enhancements to maximize the power and speed of the design.

Cache

Cache is a technology that is used to improve many aspects of computing systems. The basic idea is to use a small amount of high-speed and local memory as temporary storage. Cache can be applied in many places across a wide range of computing problems, ranging from the Internet and the World Wide Web, down to inside the CPU chip itself. All modern computer systems utilize cache in multiple places in the system.

Language Translation

We use high-level languages and human-centric graphical user interfaces (GUI) to communicate with computers. At some point, a translation must occur that converts commands into a form that the computer can understand; primitive bits that can be either 0 or 1.

Parallel Processing

One of the strategies to build machines with greater computing power is to combine many CPUs together into a single machine, and to use a technique called *parallel processing* to harness those machines to work as a team. Machines with anywhere from two to thousands of processors work together. This fascinating area includes the study of the architecture of these high-performance machines, the tools and software techniques needed to harness many machines toward one goal, and the design and development of software applications that can run on parallel computers. Theoretical models of parallel processing explore the speed-ups obtainable and the limitations of parallel processing.

Models of Computation

The functions of computers can be modeled in a number of ways using various approaches from graphical to algebraic. Some methods are complex and sophisticated, requiring significant study to become fluent in the technique. Some classical approaches model computation with an eye toward understanding whether there are limits on what can be computed (there are) and to understanding those limitations. This text provides an overview of the key concepts in computer science; this theoretical area is composed of many individually complex techniques and facets that can each require separate course(s). Consequently, theoretical areas like computation modeling and computability will be allocated only modest coverage. Two specific graphical computing model examples, finite state machines and Petri nets, are covered. These were chosen because they are easy to understand, require no mathematical tools to work, are applicable in problem solving and analysis in general, and are used in computer architecture specifically.

Artificial Intelligence

Artificial intelligence (AI) is the concept of building computers that can think for themselves. Substantial progress has been made in this area (which is highly theoretical and highly complex) by capturing human intelligence in a form that the machine can follow. It is not clear whether we have created "artificial intelligence" or simply made the machine merely mimic the way humans think. This is a fascinating area with much challenging and exciting work ahead.

Networking and the Internet

These two ideas have profoundly changed the way that we use computers and have opened up new uses for the machines in assisting humans in obtaining information. The development of the Internet, the Web (and browsers and web pages), email, and distributed computing applications has changed and enriched our lives. This area has an engineering foundation in understanding the electronics and signal processing issues that make fast communication between computers possible. This area also includes management issues; organizations now are dependent on their computers and the ability to move information from machine to machine for fast communications.

Data Structures

Data structures are techniques and strategies for organizing, storing, and accessing the data stored in a computer system. This area is technical with a theoretical flavor. Attention to efficiency, correct functioning, modifiability, and scalability are considerations in this area. An understanding of data structures and how they actually are implemented in the modern computer is critical to understanding how computers work. Data structures influence and are connected with other fields: database systems, distributed systems, efficiency, and algorithm analysis.

Computing Security

Computing security is an important field within computing that is as old as computing itself, but has received much more attention in the last decade as the proliferation of personal computers connected to the Internet has created access and opportunity for threats to our data and privacy. A theoretical direction in this field is mathematical and focuses on cryptography and the protection and security of valuable data. A more applied direction is toward managing the security process in an organization; building security plans, testing systems for vulnerabilities, and detecting and mitigating threats, and mitigation.

1.3 COMPUTING DISCIPLINES AND COMPUTING CAREERS

Computer science as a discipline is maturing. While it continues to grow and expand, it is developing new specialization areas and spawning new disciplines. Many of the new areas within computing are in interdisciplinary fields, where computer science can be applied. This fragmentation is a natural feature of a successful maturing and growing discipline. Figure 1.2 illustrates the fragmented and overlapping nature of emerging computing disciplines.

One newly emerging computing field is *applied* computer science, which focuses on areas within computer science that have direct and commonplace application. This area includes theoretical concepts, but does not emphasize theory; instead it emphasizes the ways to apply computer science. Applied computer science is a selected subset of overall computer science topics and knowledge areas, with interdisciplinary areas of computing applications. It shares some areas with the fields of information systems and software engineering.

The degree of focus on the technical science and engineering as opposed to the focus on social and business application of computing also varies along the horizontal axis. Figure 1.3 brings out this progression of social versus technical emphasis.

On the left within Figure 1.3 is computer science, which is heavily engaged in the science and engineering of computers. The theory of computing is also a part of this computer science. Moving toward the right, applied computer science deemphasizes computing theory and emphasizes applying computing in a variety of fields. Information systems require a technical understanding of computers for context but focuses on the social, behavioral, and business aspects of applying computing. The management of information systems requires only a modest understanding of the computer and its technical functions and focuses instead on the application and integration of computing technology in a business organization. Students in these fields

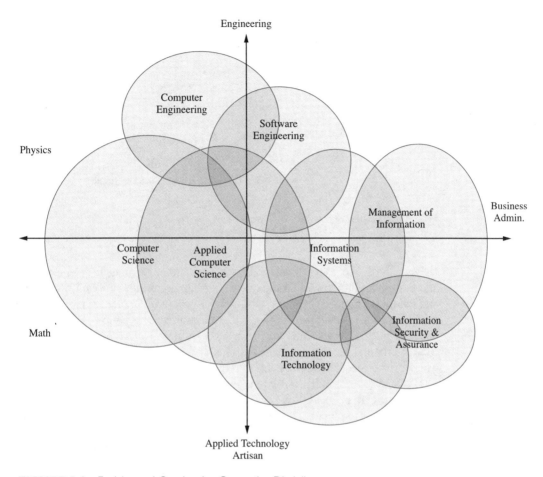

FIGURE 1.2   Evolving and Overlapping Computing Disciplines

require different levels of depth and rigor in the technical/theoretical/ engineering principles of computing and require different levels of understanding of the social sciences and business.

Two related areas that are emerging as disciplines within computing are information security and assurance and application security. The first deals with systems security, security management and planning, intrusion prevention, and detection. The latter, application security, deals with the integration of security concepts into the design of systems and applications. This is an approach that is being integrated into software engineering and design.

The application of computers and computing to many areas of human activity has opened a huge and diverse range of career options for students. The time when graduates educated in computing would spend their careers writing programs is long past. Now, graduates will design, implement, and maintain computing systems and computing networks. Software engineers and designers

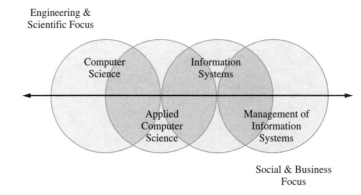

FIGURE 1.3   Discipline Focus on Technical versus Social Aspects

will manage the software development process and focus on high-level software and system architectures. Graduates will design computer simulation systems and computer games. Gradates will work for corporations managing the information assets (machines, people, data, and software systems) and develop plans for future growth and expansion and to integrate emerging technologies. Graduates will design and manage systems that are distributed across the globe, which are connected together through the Internet.

A host of computing-related and computing-dependent careers has emerged, and many traditional careers have evolved to depend heavily on computers. Interdisciplinary careers apply computing to many other traditional fields, from architecture to zoology. The student knowledgeable about computers and how to apply them will find enormous opportunities for the foreseeable future. The U.S. Bureau of Labor and Statistics predicts that employment in computing fields will be one of the fastest growing career areas of the future.[*]

1.4   EXPECTATIONS OF STUDENTS OF COMPUTER SCIENCE

In general, computer science students are expected to be able to perform at a high level in terms of tenacity and dedication as they acquire inherently complex knowledge. A competent analytical and mathematical background and ability is also required. Students must have mature and effective study skills.

However, perhaps the most important requirement for computer science students is the ability to independently solve problems: (1) The student needs the ability to analyze and understand a problem, which may itself

---

[*]http://www.bls.gov/.

require substantial study and research; (2) the student must also be able to break down a problem into components and develop a plan to solve the problem; and (3) the student must be able to bring a project to completion. In computer science, this process generally results in the synthesis of a design, a software program, or a computing system.

The requirement that students master problem-solving skills is not unique to the computer science discipline. Problem solving is one of the hallmarks of the human experience; it is one of the abilities that separate us from animals.

Applied areas in computer science are often mathematically less intense than in theoretical computer science areas, but just as easily can be as complex. Complexity is used in the computing field not just as a synonym for difficulty, but also with a more precise meaning. The sum of the number of items—components, modules, variables, and hardware, plus the number of their interactions and combinations, plus the way in which the complexity of a system grows as the system scales in size—defines the complexity of a system in the computer science arena.

For instance, a system that consists of a pail, a shovel, and a pile of sand is a simple system of only three components. However, the number of ways these pieces can be combined, plus the number of ways they can be used together, plus the number of things that can be constructed with them, multiplies the complexity of the complete system that includes not just the articles themselves, but their applications, many times over. The shovel can be used to fill the bucket to make sand-castle towers; full buckets make tall towers while partial buckets make smaller towers. The shovel can dig walls and moats to surround a sand castle. There are many ways to arrange towers and walls in a sand castle: square, rectangle, triangle, five-sided or more, nested castles within a castle, and so forth. The study of the many possible physical design layout alternatives is the study of the topology of the system.

The number of steps required to make each design varies, and the different arrangements of the steps can be more or less efficient. The study of the correctness and efficiency of instructions or recipes for building sand castles is very much like the study of program construction and algorithms.

Sand Castle Analogy

Consider building the sand castle consisting of four adjacent towers of full (pail) height illustrated in Figure 1.4.

Algorithm 1

1. Create a level space for the castle.
2. Repeat four times.
   a. Fill the bucket from the pile of sand.
   b. Upend the bucket to create a tower. Position the towers in a square pattern.
3. Repeat four times.

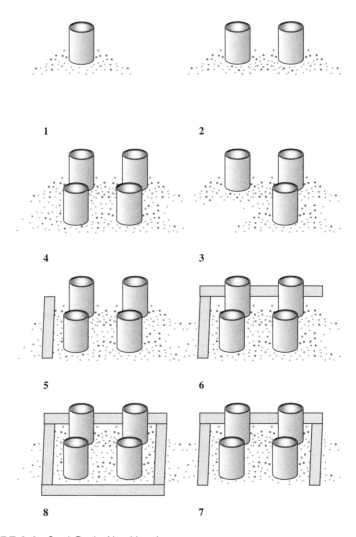

FIGURE 1.4   Sand Castle Algorithm 1

    a. Excavate a moat along one side of the towers.

Now consider the more efficient algorithm 2, illustrated in Figure 1.5.

Algorithm 2

1. Create a level space for the castle.
2. Repeat four times.
    a. Excavate a moat along one side of the future castle, placing the ex-
cavated sand in a bucket.
    b. When the bucket is full, upend it to create a tower. Position the tow-
ers in a square pattern.

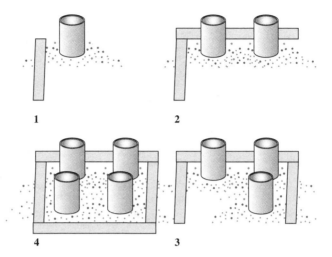

FIGURE 1.5   Sand Castle Algorithm 2

Clearly, algorithm 2 requires less work, because there is less sand to dig, since digging the moat is combined with filling the bucket for the towers. Children at play on the beach rarely consider the order of operations in their construction, unless they have built many sand castles and learned from their experience.

Software systems in particular can become extraordinarily complex, with thousands, even millions, of components and interactions that far exceed the capability of the human mind to encompass at one time. One of the preeminent themes of software engineering is the management of software complexity and software design processes that compartmentalize and minimize the apparent complexity, leading to a faster construction with fewer errors, and a more complete project.

An analytical area within computer science called algorithm analysis analyzes computer algorithms to determine their performance and complexity in relation to the number of data items that are to be processed.

Artificial intelligence includes a study of novel solutions and algorithms to a variety of difficult problems. These are often complex in terms of the number of analysis steps to be processed by the computer running the software.

It should be apparent, then, to the reader that as a computer science student, you must be interested in solving problems, thinking about solving problems, and analyzing and comparing alternative solutions and approaches and creating models and algorithms. You must also have the tenacity and persistence required to continue to work on difficult problems, even when continued progress might require a fresh start or new approach to a problem.

Because the computer is basically a simple logical machine, it and basic computer science are inherently easy to understand. The complexity and difficulty arises when we combine many layers and pieces of logic

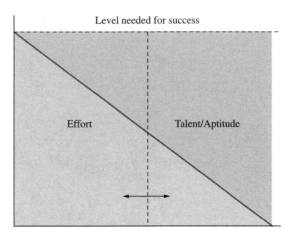

FIGURE 1.6   Success = Talent/Aptitude + Effort

and complexity into a much more complex whole that can be difficult to understand. Everyone will bring a different level of patience, tolerance for complexity, inquisitiveness, and an appreciation for the beauty of intelligent design and engineering to each task. Because people vary in their attributes and abilities, the amount of effort needed to achieve success will vary depending on each person's talent and aptitude, as illustrated in Figure 1.6.

Some readers will find that the level of effort and commitment required outweighs, for them at least, the rewards of mastering the knowledge. Others will thrive on the challenge. A quote from one of the United States' most revered presidents, Abraham Lincoln, reflects this idea:

You can be anything you want to be,
do anything you set out to accomplish,
if you hold to that desire with singleness of purpose.

1.5   MAN-VERSUS-MACHINE TRADE-OFF

This section explores the evolving cost or scarcity of computing power, generated either by humans or by computers. In the early days of computing (1940s–1960s), computing machines were extremely expensive and rare, and were used for very high-priority tasks that returned great value. Computer-processing cycles were considered to be relatively expensive and were to be hoarded and protected against waste and inefficiency.

In contrast, human effort and computing time was comparatively cheap. In fact, the early computers required the services of numerous specialists to ensure that the huge investment in computing power would return the greatest value. Systems administrators managed the system. Computer operators oversaw the flow of tasks and data into the machine and the production and storage of the results generated. Programmers were dedicated to writing computer applications and organizing the machine's processing with the highest priority placed on minimizing the computer's time and effort to accomplish a task.

Now, technology has evolved to the point where computing cycles are so inexpensive as to be almost free. No one cares that when running a personal computer capable of processing billions of instructions per second, most of that processing time is wasted while the machine sits idle or waits in between the keystrokes of even the fastest typist. Computers are so inexpensive now that they are embedded in throwaway devices and gadgets. We truly have entered the age of disposable computing.

When engineers and programmers design applications for the machines in our present age, the paramount issues are human time, time for the completion of the project in human terms, and a correctly functioning system or program. Extra processing required for the machine is a good tradeoff to minimize the human labor costs. Consequently, the techniques and philosophy for building software systems, in particular, has evolved tremendously from the early days of computing.

In order to minimize human effort and time while improving the reliability of the resulting application or software, programming languages and technologies have improved dramatically from the human point of view. Once, scientists and programmers had to learn the language of the machine at its lowest levels, in order to write code for the computer to follow. Now, we design applications and software in high-level and abstract languages, using interfaces that are convenient for us to use. These innovations require additional processing for the machine in order to translate from the human-convenient forms into a machine-usable form.

This trend and philosophy is exhibited in its most recent evolution with modern object-oriented programming languages and engineering strategies, which are constructed in part from common and reusable components. Much like the construction of automobiles that share common parts and components that are used in many different models of cars, software systems are being constructed with standardized components available on the Internet and in libraries for shared use. The inclusion of software components that may be located in cyberspace requires more effort for the machines to locate and include those common components. Still, labor costs to develop these applications and to get them working without errors (called *bugs* in software parlance) is greatly reduced—and human labor costs are the dominant cost in designing and developing new systems, not the hardware or machine costs themselves.

There was a time when software was simple enough that a designer would spend hours upon hours on a product in the design stage on paper, in order to ensure that it would be translated and run by the computer correctly the first time it was attempted. Modern computing applications have expanded so dramatically in size and power that they now exceed the capabilities of human engineers to understand in whole, and must be designed in subparts by many workers and then assembled. Now designers and engineers gladly burn computer time to test and uncover the problems flaws in their designs.

This trend is expected to continue as computers continue to become cheaper and faster and computing cycles get closer and closer to being truly "free." More and more "human computation" and effort is being off-loaded to the machine, to the point where efforts to build "artificially intelligent" machines has led to machines that mimic the way people think and act. Computer science is approaching a future when the computer can design its own systems and software with minimal input from human designers, leaving humans free for other tasks and pursuits. Whether that will occur in 10 or 50 years is a matter for speculation.

The IBM-PC

IBM (International Business Machines) had been building and marketing computers for office applications including inventory control, accounts receivable, sales analysis, and word processing stretching back to the IBM5100 of 1975, at a base price of around $9000. These machines (shown at right) were not home computers or personal computers, because their cost and lack of flexibility aimed them strictly at the small business. This low end of IBM's product line was targeted at small businesses that could not afford a larger computer mainframe or minicomputer.

IBM introduced their first version of the IBM5150 from this same product line in 1981, which became known as the IBM Personal Computer (IBM-PC). This machine evolved from the 5100 series and continued the line of applications for small business. The IBM5150 included a monochrome monitor; zero, one, or two floppy disk drives; and could be connected to a printer. Unlike the previous machines in the 5100 series, the 5150 included the ability to connect joysticks for computer games, included a BASIC program interpreter, and included a flexible operating system similar to that which was in use in many home computers (CP/M Control Program for Microcomputers), making the machine suitable for home computing. That operating system was created by Tim Paterson of Seattle Computer Products as QDOS (Quick and Dirty Operating System), which was licensed to Microsoft, which had the contract to supply one of the three operating system options for the 5150.

The IBM-PC used a number of off-the-shelf components that kept the cost down ($1565) and included an open bus specification that allowed other hardware manufacturers to build devices and boards for the machine that could be plugged into slots in the motherboard.

Even though the machine was both very expensive and very limited in capabilities compared to other home computers, the IBM nameplate brought the machine respectability in the business marketplace. Purchasing a home computer known for its gaming capabilities was a difficult justification for a business manager, but purchasing an IBM5150 computer (even if more expensive) did not carry the same connotations. The IBM5150 Personal Computer was a strong success in the marketplace for business computers.

The acceptance of the IBM5150 in the business world opened opportunities for software developers to design programs for business applications, with a market capable of paying serious bucks for software, which lead to many new software start-ups to supply programs for the machine. This explosion of software applications in turn contributed to the success of the IBM-PC.

The open bus design, the use of an operating system similar to the standard OS in use for home computers, and the IBM nameplate were the key elements that lead to the IBM-PC platform architecture becoming the standard for personal computers.

1.6   EVOLUTION OF THE COMPUTER

The computer evolved from mechanical calculation aids like the abacus and from manufacturing control concepts like punched cards for tabulating the census and pattern controls for automatic looms and player pianos.

The development of the modern digital computer is the work of many scientists and engineers in many countries, with theoretical origins dating back to the ancient China. No one country or researcher can be said to have developed the computer. Table 1.1 illustrates the international origins of the computer.

An early mechanical computer of sorts was designed by Charles Babbage in the 1800s that was based on mechanical calculators. The desire to automate tedious calculations for speed and greater accuracy has been of great interest in the sciences and military.

Charles Babbage (1791–1871)

Babbage was a mathematician and engineer who originated the idea of a programmable computer. He developed a mechanical calculator, and later designed a mechanical difference engine with a separate data and program memory and a sophisticated control unit capable of making conditional jumps within the program.

TABLE 1.1   International Contributions in Computing

Contribution	Date	Scientist	Country	Ref
Chinese Abacus Decimal Counting Device	202 BC		China	
Antikythera Mechanism Mechanical (gears) analog astronomy computer	100 BC	Posidonious	Greece	
Napier's Bones Calculator using rods and a board	1617	John Napier	Scotland	
Calculating Clock Mechanical automatic calculator, used by Johannes Kepler	1623	Wilhelm Schickard	Germany	
Pascalina Mechanical calculator	1642	Blaise Pascal	France	
Binary Number System	1705	Gottfried Leibniz	Germany	Ch. 3
Analytical Engine Mechanical programmable computer	1822	Charles Babbage	England	
Programming Programming for Babbages's analytical engine	1843	Ada Lovelace	England	
Boolean Algebra	1847	George Boole	England	
Z3 Computer	1941	Konrad Zuse	Germany	
ABC Computer	1941	John Atanasoff	USA	
Colossus Computer	1943	Tommy Flowers	UK	
Harvard Architecture	1943	Howard Aiken –IBM	USA	
Von Neumann—Architecture	1945	John Von Neumann	Hungary/USA	
Transistor	1950	William Schockley	USA	
Integrated Circuit	1952 1959	G.W.A Dummer Jack Kilby/Texas Instruments	England USA	

(continued)

TABLE 1.1 International Contributions in Computing (continued)

Contribution	Date	Scientist	Country	Ref
FORTRAN programming language	1956	John W. Backus—IBM	USA	
Database	1963	Charles Bachman	USA	
Cache	1965	M.V. Wilkes	England	
Internet (ARPANET)	1969	Lawrence Roberts	USA	
UNIX operating systems	1970	Ken Thomson Dennis Ritchie	USA	
C programming language	1972	Dennis Ritchie	USA	
Windowing GUI	1973	Xerox PARC	USA	
Personal Computer—Micral	1973	Philippe Kahn	France	
IBM PC	1981	IBM	USA	
World Wide Web	1990	Tim Berners-Lee	England	
Linux operating system	1991	Linus Torvalds	Finland	
Java programming language	1995	James Gosling—SUN	USA	

Early applications of the first computers were used in the military to calculate artillery shell trajectories in order to build highly accurate firing tables. The military also needed high-speed calculating machines for code-breaking and encryption. In World War II, Germany used a mechanical cipher system to protect and encrypt their radio transmissions. The system used a set of wheels that could be keyed. The number of possible combinations of wheel alignments meant that simply trying combinations would not lead to solutions. During the same time period, a need for automated calculation machine arose during the effort to build the first atomic bomb. In that project, scores of human calculators were employed to work the math, with double and triple checking of results.

Early Experimental Computers

Early experiments in building a computer were conducted independently by a number of scientists/engineers in various countries, some funded as part of the World War II effort. The design of the Electronic Numerical Integrator and Computer (ENIAC) borrowed concepts from the

FIGURE 1.7   Atanasoff–Berry Computer Replica at Iowa State University

Atanasoff–Berry computer (ABC) at Iowa State University (Figure 1.7). Table 1.2 lists early computer research efforts.

The First Generation Of Modern Commercial Computers

This period continued from the mid 1940s until around 1958. The first machines of this period were constructed from vacuum tubes (like light bulbs with electrical switching capabilities). These machines were extremely large, occupying very large rooms just for the hardware. The vacuum-tube technology was unreliable (remember, light bulbs with filaments in them burn out) and required a great deal of power to operate. Many people were required to operate and maintain the machines.

The first machines were "programmed" by rewiring the connections inside the machine, a tedious process. Therefore, having a single machine run more than one program at a time was impossibtrle. These early machines were capable of around 40,000 operations per second (Figure 1.8).

TABLE 1.2 Early Computers

Date	Scientist	Country	Name	Programmable	Binary	Electronic
May 1941	Conrad Zuse	Germany	Z3	Punched film	Yes	No
Summer 1941	John Atanasoff	Germany/USA	ABC	No	Yes	Yes
1943	Tommy Flowers	UK	Colossus	By rewiring	Yes	Yes
1944	Howard Aiken/IBM	USA	Harvard Mark I	Punched paper Tape	No	No
1944	Mauchly & Eckert	USA	ENIAC	By rewiring	No	Yes

FIGURE 1.8 IBM Mark I Computer

Second-Generation Computers

This era covered the period from 1958 to 1964. This was a time of major advances in computing, including the use of the transistor to replace the vacuum tubes and the stored-program technology and machine language programming that enabled the avoidance of hard wiring the machine for each new task.

The *transistor* is a solid-state device, meaning that there is no filament in a tube that heats up and can burn out. The transistor is much faster, more reliable, uses much less power, and is much smaller than a vacuum tube. This scientific and engineering advance represented by the development and use of the transistor allowed computers to grow in computing power and speed.

The invention of the "stored program" concept was critical: A program stored in electronic memory replaced the hard-wired connections that determine what program the computer runs. Changing the wired connections allowed the computer to be a general-purpose machine, capable of many different tasks and able to perform many different functions. Earlier computers could not grow in power due to the need to run wires to a central switchboard where a group of specialists would change wiring connections by hand.

These early machines were called *mainframes* because a set of components were assembled onto boards where they were installed in a large metal frame. Machines of this period were capable of hundreds of thousands of operations per second.

Third-Generation Computers

Machines of this era (1965–1971) continued to be constructed using transistors, but now the technology for manufacturing transistors had advanced to the point where many transistors could be integrated on a single chip. This advance dramatically reduced the size of the transistors, reduced the amount of power required, and allowed them to run much faster.

The software advances during this period included the development of high-level programming languages. High-level languages allow the programmer to work with a much more human-friendly language and increased the speed and reliability of the programming process. This allowed much larger and more complex programs and applications to be created.

Initially, there was a noticeable trade-off in performance. The high-level language programs that were translated into machine language so the computer could run them lost some efficiency as compared to programs written directly in low-level code. The efficiency of the translation process (compilers and interpreters) has greatly improved since this period. The use of high-level languages is an example of trading more computer work and effort to save human work and effort and time.

Computers of this era proliferated into many business enterprises for managing budgets and finance. Machines of this period were capable of a million operations per second.

Fourth-Generation Computers

Fourth-generation computers (1971–1995) are identified by the use of very-large-scale integrated chips, the widespread introduction of the personal computer, and the networking of computers. Fourth-generation computing saw a huge proliferation of machines, with affordable computers based on microprocessors. Microprocessors integrate an entire CPU on a single chip, and their entrance into the marketplace allowed computers to be owned and operated by the consumer.

This personal computer allowed every individual to be his or her own computing center, empowering computer users to work independently of a large high-cost computing center under centralized control. Applications on personal computers thrived in diverse areas from games and entertainment to database, word-processing, and spreadsheet applications.

Large high-performance machines of this era could process a hundred million operations per second or more, whereas early microprocessors were capable of a million or so operations per second.

The dramatically increasing computing power and its proliferation supported the first practical applications of artificial intelligence (AI) running on microprocessors. These first AI applications captured human expertise as data and software, allowing the computer to follow the same set of rules and logic that a human expect would, thereby "capturing" the human expertise in a machine form.

The availability of cheap and easy-to-use microprocessors allowed computers to be embedded in many other devices. The modern automobile is a system that has many processors working together to achieve higher automotive performance and to add previously impossible capabilities like active suspensions, vehicle stability systems, and braking management systems.

The embedding of microprocessors in machines made practical the construction of robots that are now used extensively in manufacturing and for other purposes.

Fifth-Generation Computers

This is the current generation of computers (mid 1990s to present), and its hallmark is the use of machines distributed geographically but linked together using the Internet. Examples include:

- **World wide web:** Using a personal computer to search for and display information that is stored and managed on thousands of machines distributed around the world. The Web is also used for electronic commerce, where consumers can order and purchase merchandise by means of the computer from anywhere in the world.

- **Distributed object technologies:** This concept allows programs to be constructed from components, and the components can be located anywhere accessible on the Internet. This maximizes the use of reusable code, so applications can be constructed from existing building blocks and assembled into a whole. This strategy includes the ability for a running program to search for and find the program module somewhere in "cyberspace" on the Internet without the user being aware of all the behind-the-scenes activities.
- **Middleware:** This is an application design concept for building software applications that are distributed across a network and constructed in layers or tiers. Each tier performs a different function. There is a client tier—the user's PC—which runs the user interface and does a modest amount of preprocessing. There is often a back-end tier where the applications accesses data stored in a database that could itself be distributed across multiple machines. There is at least one middle layer or tier that does a portion of the overall processing or work involved. There is often a tier dedicated to creating dynamic html (hyper-text markup language) pages that can be viewed by the user on a standard Internet browser, that are created specifically and exist temporarily for one user's specific request for information or commands to be processed.
- **Grid computing:** Grid computing is the concept of creating a grid of computing power. Just as consumers plug appliances into an electrical grid for electrical power, grid computing customers can tap into the amount of supercomputing power that they need. Participants contributed their high-performance machines to the grid to share with others, and may then tap into the power of all the machines on the grid. The challenge in building a grid is designing software "middleware" to solve a number of problems:
  1. A security layer to control access to the grid.
  2. Workload distribution algorithms that are needed to balance the load across the machines in the grid.
  3. Application loading and distribution algorithms are needed to allow new applications to be written for the grid that can then be "automatically" without having to install software individually on each machine in the grid.

Machines of this current computing generation are capable of billions of operations per second and supercomputers are capable of even more; however, the hallmark of this generation is not the continued advance in processor design and manufacturing (which is in fact, continuing) but the novel ways that people use networked and connected computing machines to build distributed computing systems interconnected over the Internet.

Trends for the Future

The next evolution of embedding or integrating microprocessors within larger systems is leading to integrating microprocessors within the human body to replace or enhance human functions. One example is to assist people with prosthetic limbs, artificial limbs that function more like the biological originals. Medical scientists are teaming with computer engineers to build implantable insulin pumps, heart function monitoring devices and pacemakers, and primitive artificial vision devices.

High-performance computing is proceeding on three fronts:

1. Completing the development of grid computer systems.
2. Continued enhancement of individual computers with additional processors and processing elements in a single machine. Multiple processor computers and multi-(processor)core machines are currently available.
3. Quantum computing will build computer logic at a lower level than our current machines. Instead of manipulating electrons to store and transmit data, quantum computers will use the subatomic physics of quantum particles to store and manipulate data. This technology is under development and might be common by 2020.

CHAPTER 1 QUESTIONS

1. Consider your own problem-solving skills. What problem-solving activity have you participated in that seems similar to the problem solving for computing problems?

2. Develop your own algorithm for building a four-tower sand castle, and then compare your algorithm to both algorithms 1 and 2 in Section 1.4.

3. Algorithms can contain conditions and checkpoints that can add or replace steps, or even change the order of steps. The sand castle example is very simple and contains no internal decision points. A more complex algorithm could check if the sand is moist enough to hold its shape. If not, then a small amount of water can be added to the sand to make it "sticky." Construct a revised sand castle algorithm that includes checking to see if the sand has enough moisture to hold its shape and adding water if needed.

4. Choose one area or specialized field within computing that seems interesting, and research that area on the Internet. Write a short one- or two-paragraph description of that area.

5. Consider how computing technology has changed lives. Choose one innovation that has occurred within your lifetime, research the evolution of this technology, and write a short paragraph describing the technology and its impact.

The Computer System and Basic Instruction Processing Function

C hapter 2 explains what a computer is and does and dissects the machine into its major component parts. **Prerequisite knowledge needed:** No specific knowledge needed, but an ability to think logically and to understand a complex machine.

2.0 INTRODUCTION

The computer is a machine that follows instructions written by humans. It has no inherent intelligence of its own (at present), but follows "captured" human intelligence that has been rendered into a form the machine can follow.

The machine itself is primarily electronic, with the movement and storage of electricity and electric charges representing data and information. As the data (electrical values) flow through the computer system, they can be changed and manipulated according to mechanical rules that the computer must follow. Those rules are created and designed by human intelligence.

This chapter examines the construction of a computer system by dissecting the machine to its fundamental components, and examining the construction of those components and how they work together.

John (Janos) Von Neumann (1903–1957)

Von Neumann was a prominent mathematician who made many contributions in areas, including quantum physics, functional analysis, set theory, game theory, and computer science. Von Neumann was a pioneer of the modern digital computer, one of the original members of the Institute for Advanced Study at Princeton, and a member of the Manhattan Project.

Von Neumann devised an architecture for a digital computer that is the basic template for virtually all computing machines in use today, though with enhancements for better performance. His concept of a "stored-program computer," where the program itself is not wired in the hardware of the machine but exists as software stored separately in memory, is a key design concept.

2.1 BASIC SYSTEM COMPONENTS

Examining a computer system from a high-level point of view reveals that a computer has six basic components or categories of components:

1. **CPU:** The central processing unit. In common usage, this term is often used to describe the box or enclosure within which the computer components reside. To a computer scientist, the CPU is the processor chip that can interpret and execute the instructions in a computer program (software).

2. **Main memory** (also called primary storage): This is working storage for programs and information, which is used while the computer is powered on and running. The main memory is generally not permanent or fixed storage; its contents are wiped clean when the machine is powered down.

3. **Storage** (also called secondary storage): This term covers a variety of types of devices to store and retrieve data, information, and software programs. Devices range in speed, amount of storage, and cost. These can include hard drives, floppy drives, RAM drives, compact discs (CDs), memory sticks, secure digital (SD) cards, and so forth.

4. **Input/output devices:** This is a category of devices used to provide input to the machine, display output for the user, or to communicate with other computers. Devices in this category include the computer monitor, keyboard, mouse, network card, modem, camera, printers, scanners, and the like.

5. **Bus:** An electrical "highway" that is used to connect the components. The bus is multiple wires, so that many bits can be communicated between devices at the same time. It is typical for a computer system to have two or more buses.

6. **Operating system:** This is the software program that makes the computing hardware usable. The operating system includes low-level software for controlling the hardware devices, as well as software for managing programs and the resources in the computer system. The operating system includes software that provides a user interface into the system. This is typically a graphical user interface (GUI), though other types of interfaces are possible. The operating system also generally provides a programming interface; i.e., a way for programmers to utilize portions of the operating system routines when developing software. Most of the operating system is software, which resides in secondary storage and is loaded into the computer's memory when the computer boots up. Usually, small portion of system code is stored in hardware in a chip, and may be called a basic input-output system (BIOS), which contains instructions for loading and starting the operating system.

John V. Atanasoff (1903–1995)

Professor of Physics at Iowa State University Dr. John Atanasoff and his student Clifford Berry developed an electronic digital computer in 1939 and a full-scale version in 1942. The machine was not general purpose and lacked program control, but it was based on the binary system, Boolean algebra, and was implemented with vacuum tubes. John Mauchly, codesigner of the ENIAC computer, visited Atanasoff's labs and viewed his machine and writings as a prelude to developing the ENIAC. Atanasoff was recognized as the true inventor of the electronic digital computer in a patent dispute, based on the link between his ABC machine and the development of the ENIAC.

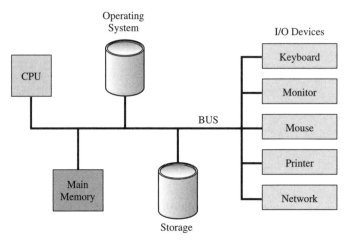

FIGURE 2.1   Computer System Components

Figure 2.1 illustrates a high-level diagram of a simple computing system. It shows the operating system and storage separately, though the operating system is software that resides on a storage device (usually a hard-disk drive) that is also used to store software applications and data. The other storage device (labeled "storage" in the figure) represents optional hard-disk drives, but also optical drives, floppy drives, memory sticks, SD cards, and other storage device technologies.

IBM

Founded in 1911 as the Calculating-Tabulating-Recording Company to manufacture and market commercial scales, time recorders, and card tabulation machines, International Business Machines (IBM) has since grown to be one of the world's largest corporations and a leader in computer systems and computer research.

2.2   THE CENTRAL PROCESSING UNIT

The central processing unit (CPU) is the part of the computer system that contains the logic used to execute or process instructions, which then cause the computer do work. The CPU is a single chip that is the master of all the other devices in the system and any secondary processors.

The CPU chip itself is quite small—the size of a fingernail or smaller. Because it is enveloped in a plastic or ceramic package, the CPU chip, when handled, appears larger, perhaps a square inch in size. The ceramic enclo-

FIGURE 2.2   Personal Computer Motherboard with Fan-Cooled CPU

sure around the CPU chip protects the fragile CPU, connects input and output wires to pins on the chip for easy connection to the rest of the computer system, and is involved in transferring waste heat away from the chip. Depending on how fast the CPU operates, many chips can generate sufficient heat to cause internal failures unless the excess heat is dealt with in some way with fans and radiator fins (Figure 2.2).

Inside the CPU, everything is stored as numbers. The meaning or interpretation of these numbers depends on what information is being stored: video recordings, sound files, graphic images, words and text, and of course mathematical or accounting numbers. All these types of information are stored as data inside the computer using binary numbers.

The binary number system has only two digits: 0 and 1. This two-digit system turns out to be convenient to build and manufacture using modern digital electronics technologies. A binary representation of the number 18, for instance, looks like this:

10010

All information that we manipulate with computers, including names, pictures and music, must be translated at some point by the computer and

FIGURE 2.3 Underside of CPU Chip and Socket

computer software into simple binary representations. This translation can occur at a number of different times using a small number of ways to represent data and information in binary digits (0, 1) called *bits*. The CPU operates on values represented as binary digits, and in fact, has no "knowledge" about the meaning of the binary numbers or what they represent in the human world. It simple-mindedly manipulates the data represented by binary numbers as it is told to do so by its programs—which are themselves also translated or converted into binary representations before the computer can work with them. The computer itself has no intelligence of its own, and all of its abilities are simply the result of capturing the intelligence and logic of its makers (both hardware designers and software programmers).

A simple CPU contains three basic components. Modern advanced processors blur these distinct components and include additional performance-enhancing features, but the three primary components of a simple CPU are:

1. **Registers:** A set of temporary storage locations for numbers while the CPU is working with them. If the intention is to add two numbers together, usually each number would first be loaded from memory into a register, prior to adding them together. Then, the result of the addition might be stored temporarily in a register, prior to being stored back to the computer's main memory. The CPU can act upon the data stored in

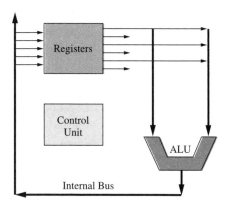

FIGURE 2.4 CPU Internals

its internal registers much more quickly than if it was to work directly with data stored in memory.

2. **Arithmetic logic unit (ALU):** This is the logic that can do operations with binary numbers. In addition to basic math functions like addition, subtraction, multiplication, and division, the ALU can also manipulate numbers in other ways and compare numbers together for equality and inequalities (greater than, less than, or equal to).

3. **Control unit:** This component is the logic that is written into the hardware chip that determines the sequence of events needed to process instructions. Things like how to decode an instruction, how to move data from one register to the ALU, where to put results from the ALU, and which instruction should be processed next are all functions that are encoded in the CPU chip as part of the control logic or control unit of the processor.

Figure 2.4 illustrates the internal architecture of the CPU including the registers, ALU, control unit, and internal buses.

Note in Figure 2.4 that data flows through the CPU in a cycle, from registers to the ALU, where values are processed, and then the result flows back to a be stored in a register.

2.3 COMPUTER INSTRUCTION

The computer is a machine that processes instructions. Each single instruction does only a very small task, but the computer can process instructions at such a high rate of speed (millions to billions of instructions per second) that the computer can perform a tremendous quantity of computing work in a short period of time. At the lowest level, computer instructions are represented as numbers stored using the binary number system. The computer's

CPU must examine each instruction that is to be processed in order to determine what function must be performed (i.e., math operation or another) and what data will be manipulated. This process is called *decoding the instruction*.

The following is a representative assembly-language instruction that adds the contents of two registers together. This operation is abbreviated with **ADR**, which means to **AD**d **R**egisters.

    ADR R1 R2

Assembly language is a low-level programming language that is closely associated with the machine language that the computer "understands," if it can be said to understand anything as a simple-minded instruction following machine. The assembly language code can be directly translated (by an assembler program) into machine code which the computer then can process:

    010000 0001 0010

The computer is designed to process machine-code instructions that are hard for humans to work with. The difficulty of machine-code programming lead to the creation of assembly language. Assembly language is much easier to work with than machine code, but even assembly is too close to the complexity of the computer hardware, and it is difficult and tedious to work with. Consequently, even higher level programming languages have been developed and are in use. This is an example of shifting work from the human programmer to the machine, because the higher-level languages require more computer time to convert to machine-readable form, but the trade-off is worth it.

Machine code and assembly language are organized in an instruction format, with fields that indicate the operation to be performed (operation code, shortened to OpCode or Op), and operands on which the instruction will operate (R1 and R2 are registers).

In Figure 2.5, there are fields for the operation code (Op) and two operands (registers R1 and R2). The operation code specifies what operation is to be done, and the operands hold the data that is to be manipulated or modified.

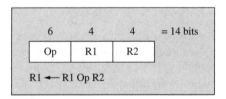

FIGURE 2.5 Simple Instruction Format

Konrad Zuse (1910–1995)

Zuse was a German engineer and computer pioneer who built the first tape-stored-program computer, the Z3, in 1941, developed the first high-level programming language, and founded the first computer startup to market the Z4 computer in 1946. IBM purchased options on his patents in 1946. Zuse's Z22 was the first digital computer to utilize magnetic memory.

In 1969, Zuse published a physics/metaphysical view of the universe (*Calculating Space*) as being computed by some virtual computing grid that explains the operations of the fundamental physical laws. The concept has received recent serious consideration, including a 2002 book by Mathematica developer Stephan Wolfram called *A New Kind of Science*.

2.4 FETCH/DECODE/EXECUTE/ INTERRUPT CYCLE

The computer is a digital and electronic machine that processes instructions. Both the instructions themselves and the logic that is needed to process those instructions should be considered to be "captured" human intelligence and logic that has been incorporated into a machine. The logic that is needed to process computer instructions can be quite complex. As an introduction, the following explains the cycle that the CPU repeats millions or billions of times per second in executing instructions.

1. **Instruction fetch:** The next instruction to be process by the CPU must be fetched from the memory into the CPU, where it is stored in a register expressly designed to hold instructions. Fetching an instruction generally requires a single cycle. On some systems with extremely large instruction formats, a number of processor/bus cycles may be required to fetch an instruction, depending on the width of the instruction and the width of the bus, which is measured in bits. The logic to do the instruction fetch is part of the control unit of the CPU.
2. **Instruction decode:** Determines what the instruction is supposed to do, and in particular, what operation or manipulation will be performed on the data, and what operands (data) are required before the instruction can execute. Usually, operands will be required to be loaded into registers in the CPU.
3. **Operand fetch:** Operands that are not already stored in CPU registers may be loaded from memory into registers. If multiple operands are required for the instruction, some computer systems may require multiple fetches from memory to registers. The number of operands that are al-

lowed, and whether they must be loaded into registers inside the CPU or may reside in memory, are key design points in building processor chips. The control unit has the logic needed to fetch operands from memory and store them in registers.

4. **Instruction execution:** After all operands are ready and the operation is to be performed has been determined, this phase of the instruction execution cycle executes the operation on the operands. The CPU control unit instructs the arithmetic logic unit (ALU) to execute the operation on the operands.

5. **Check for interrupts:** The last phase in the cycle has the CPU pausing before executing the next instruction to check for signals requesting the CPU's attention. Other devices, events, or inputs may require processing by the CPU, forcing the CPU to interrupt the current program it is executing in order to do other things. When a CPU "services" an interrupt, it first saves its place in its current processing, then switches to running other programs and instructions to service the interrupt. Then, after the needed processing is complete, the CPU returns to the "saved place" in its processing and picks up where it left off.

Figure 2.6 illustrates this instruction execution cycle and also illustrates another important idea: Some stages in the cycle are handled internally within the CPU chip itself, while other stages require communication with memory or other devices in the computer. When communication between the CPU and other devices is required, a bus is used to communicate signals and data in bits. That bus is shared by all devices in the computer system and has the potential to be a bottleneck. The bus can handle only one request at a time, and only one device in the computer can use the bus at a time.

2.5   SIMPLE COMPUTER INSTRUCTIONS

Consider the simple computing function of adding two numbers together. The numbers to be added (operands) are stored in the computer's memory. The result that is to be computed also must be stored into memory. For the CPU to do the addition, the operands must first be copied from memory into registers.

```
LOAD  R1  Num1
LOAD  R2  Num2
ADR   R1  R2
```

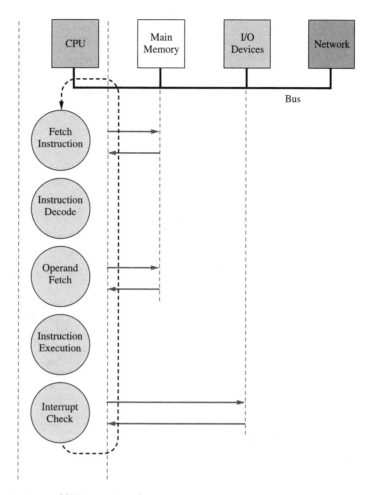

FIGURE 2.6 CPU Instruction Cycle

```
STOR R1 Result
```

The initial state of the computer system prior to executing any of these instructions is as follows:

Register 1 empty
Register 2 empty
Number 1 = 4
Number 2 = 5
Result empty

The current "state" of the computer system can be conveniently displayed in tables such as the ones shown in Figure 2.7, which show both the contents of the CPU's registers and the contents of memory:

FIGURE 2.7 Initial State of the CPU and Memory

CPU	
Register	Contents
R1	
R2	

Memory	
Location	Contents
Num1	4
Num2	5
Result	

Figure 2.8 shows the tables after executing the first instruction: `LOAD R1 Num1`:

FIGURE 2.8 State after Executing the First Instruction

CPU	
Register	Contents
R1	**4**
R2	

Memory	
Location	Contents
Num1	**4**
Num2	5
Result	

Figure 2.9 shows the tables after executing the second instruction: `LOAD R2 Num2`:

FIGURE 2.9 State after Executing the Second Instruction

CPU	
Register	Contents
R1	4
R2	**5**

Memory	
Location	Contents
Num1	4
Num2	5
Result	

Figure 2.10 shows the tables after executing the third instruction: ADR R1 R2:

FIGURE 2.10
State after Executing the Third Instruction

CPU		Memory	
Register	Contents	Location	Contents
R1	**9**	Num1	4
R2	**5**	Num2	5
		Result	

Note that the sum overwrites the original contents of register R1. Registers are used for temporary storage.

Figure 2.11 shows the tables after executing the fourth instruction: STOR R1 Result:

FIGURE 2.11
State after Executing the Fourth Instruction

CPU		Memory	
Register	Contents	Location	Contents
R1	**9**	Num1	4
R2	5	Num2	5
		Result	**9**

The example illustrated in the previous figures shows that a number of instructions are required to accomplish a modest amount of work. Some operations may even require substantially more instructions than this simple addition example. The power of the computer lies in its ability to process billions of instructions per second, each doing only a small portion of a task, but because so many instructions can be completed in a small amount of time, the computer can be extremely powerful.

The previous example also illustrates low-level programming functions in an assembly language programming. Programming at this level is painstaking and tedious, so we have developed higher-level languages that make the process easier and less trying for human programmers. In high-level languages, a single instruction can be written that accomplishes the work of the four assembly instructions in the example:

```
LOAD R1 Num1
LOAD R2 Num2
ADR R1 R2
STOR R1 Result
```

These four instructions can be accomplished in a high-level language with a single instruction or programming statement:

```
Result = Num1 + Num2
```

2.6   COMPUTER ARCHITECTURE LAYERS

A computer system can be viewed as being composed of a set of layers of functionality. This conceptual point of view of examining complex systems in layers is used in many areas of computing. This decomposition-by-layer technique is used in building and analyzing networking protocols, building and configuring operating systems, building and integrating multitiered computer systems and grid computer systems (explained in a later chapter), and in the development of application programs. It is just one way to apply the divide-and-conquer approach to problem solving that allows us to look at small portion of a large and complex system, and then understand and design each portion individually.

In computer architecture, each layer is constructed on top of the layer before it; each layer then becomes a foundation for the layers that are created on top of it (Figure 2.12). The complexity and details of the foundational layers that are below any given layer are abstracted for the layers built above it. In this way, the complexity and details can be "black boxed" (hidden within a box that conceals its contents) in order to focus on the current layer and its mechanics. Each layer uses the constructions of the previous layers as building blocks to support the new layer's construction.

This approach is similar to that used in software design, and the point is the same: managing the complexity of the system and design. The following layers create a computing system.

1. **Transistors and gates:** constructing small devices called logic gates from transistors.
2. **Simple devices:** building simple, elemental devices using gates as the construction components.

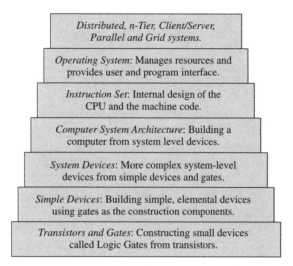

Distributed, n-Tier, Client/Server, Parallel and Grid systems.

Operating System: Manages resources and provides user and program interface.

Instruction Set: Internal design of the CPU and the machine code.

Computer System Architecture: Building a computer from system level devices.

System Devices: More complex system-level devices from simple devices and gates.

Simple Devices: Building simple, elemental devices using gates as the construction components.

Transistors and Gates: Constructing small devices called Logic Gates from transistors.

FIGURE 2.12 Computer System Design Layers

3. **System devices:** building more complex devices (like registers, comparators, and memory) from simple devices.
4. **Computer system architecture and components:** building a computer from system-level devices.
5. **Instruction set:** specifying the CPU's internal architecture and capabilities with the instruction set. The instruction set specifies the programmer's interface to the hardware, in both machine code and assembly language.
6. **Operating systems:** provides basic functionality to the device, a user interface to the computer system, and a programmer's interface to the system.
7. **Distributed, *n*-tier, client/server and parallel systems:** interconnecting many computing systems together to work cooperatively.

The understanding of each of the layers of a computer system and the interdependencies of the layers is the foundation for understanding and comparing different computer system designs. Note that there are architectural designs at multiple levels in a computer:

- Architecture of the CPU
- Architecture of the computer system
- Architecture of the operating system
- Architecture of the computing applications
- Architecture of the interconnections linking one computing system to many others

Each of these different layers represents a different focus of study with separate courses and research tracks in each area.

2.7   OPERATING SYSTEMS

The operating system provides extremely important functions that convert a set of computing hardware into a usable system:

- Manage the resources of the computer system
- Provide a user interface
- Provide a programming interface
- Provide a networking interface

Manage the Resources of the Computer System

Disk space, input/output devices, and CPU-processing time are resources that need to be managed efficiently and effectively. The operating system provides a mechanism for organizing the data storage for efficient access. Secondary storage is organized in order to make the efficient use of the available space but also to maximize performance by minimizing the physical movement of components inside the disk drive. Disk drives contain read/write heads that float above the surface of the disk and must be moved back and forth over the disk surface. Because physically moving this component is very slow compared to the speed of the other parts of a computer system, it is critical to overall performance to organize the storage to minimize this drag on performance. An efficient mechanism for labeling files on the disk, indexing files, and locating files is provided by the operating system.

The computer consists of a number of input and output devices, from disk drives to monitors to printers and network interfaces. Each of these devices requires access and control through a defined process. The operating system contains device–driver software specific to each hardware device. The operating system also controls which process or user program is granted access to specific devices and manages that overall process to avoid conflicts and interference.

Managing the CPU processing is particularly interesting when the computer can run multiple processes and support multiple users on the system at the same time. A strategy that allocates CPU time in small pieces to each running process is called *time slicing* and allows the user to multitask. The strategies and algorithms devised to accomplish this critical function are particularly intriguing because they must perform their function efficiently, fairly, and without wasting processing time. The role of the operating system in a computer system is illustrated in Figure 2.13.

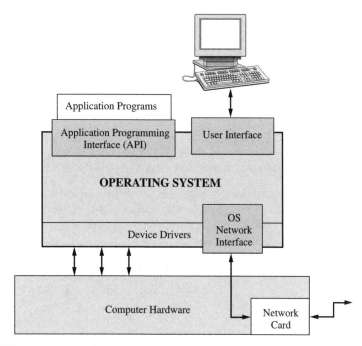

FIGURE 2.13   Role of the Operating System

Provide a User Interface

Users must have a way to interact with the computer and the software applications. This is accomplished through a software component that is part of the operating system. The simplest form of user interface is a command-line interface, which allows the user to type (or speak) commands to the system. The user must know the language and syntax for providing commands, which can be arcane and complex at times. A more user-friendly interface that demands less of the user is the graphical user interface (GUI), which provides a kind of virtual world with pictures and graphics that the user can manipulate and interact with to control the system. More recent investigations have extended this concept through the development of a virtual environment and interface designed to allow humans to interact with the machines similarly to the way that we interact with other people and objects in our daily living.

The objective behind this design trend is to make this human–computer interaction (HCI) simpler and more natural and intuitive, shifting more of the communication effort from the human to the machine. The command-line interface requires that humans study and learn a language that the computer can understand (more work for us), while a virtual interface is software and hardware that handles the translation effort for us. In all cases, the user interface insulates the human users from the internal complexities of the computer.

The strategic decisions of where to place the work/effort and complexity between the main components of a system—human users, software, and hardware—is a pervasively interesting question in computing. The specific allocations of this effort fluctuate with technological developments and ever-greater demands and uses for computing systems. The general trend is to shift work and complexity from humans to software, and from software to hardware.

Provide a Programming Interface

The operating system contains the software code needed to interact with the hardware systems in the computer. Applications software should use this system software to access resources in a controlled fashion, so the operating system must provide a way for applications to hook into these services. Often called the API (application programming interface), the OS manufacturer provides a defined interface as a set of modules or functions that can be called from within program software.

Provide a Networking Interface

Computers are networked together through local area networks (LANs) and the Internet to allow users to exchange information and access programs and resources on other machines. The software to manage the network interface unit (NIU) and to control access to the Internet and to provide a World Wide Web browser as a user interface, has been incorporated into and integrated with the operating system. The programming interface (API) also includes a way for software to access networked resources and the Internet through operating system-provided functions.

CHAPTER 2 QUESTIONS

1. Explain the architecture layer concept and why it is useful to view computer systems using this conceptual model.
2. List and describe the basic components of a computer system.
3. Describe the role of the CPU in a computer system.
4. Explain the cycle that a CPU goes through in executing instructions.
5. Explain what the ADR instruction of Section 2.3 does.
6. If you were to add a subtract instruction to the simple programming instructions of Section 2.5, explain in detail what your instruction would do.

7. Draw a diagram like those shown in Section 2.5, showing a simple computer system with three registers containing the numbers 3, 5, and 7, and three memory locations containing the number 2, 4, and 8.

8. Design a program of simple computer instructions (as in Section 2.5) that will add two numbers together that are stored in memory locations named NUM2 and NUM3 and put the result of the addition into memory at the location labeled NUM1.

Programming

C hapter 3 is an introduction to the concepts of computer programming. This chapter is not an introduction to a specific programming language or a tutorial on how to program with a coverage of syntax, but is instead an overview and summary of computer programming concepts. Each different programming language has its own set of keywords for specific functions and operations and has its own syntax and grammar for arranging programming statements (instructions) and multiple statements together.

This overview presents common ideas that are universal to computer programming and introduces programming concepts using pseudocode and flowcharts.

Prerequisite knowledge needed: The student must be familiar with a computer system, what it does, and how it functions in general, and the idea that the computer as a machine follows instructions. This knowledge is contained in Chapter 2.

Lady Ada Lovelace (1815–1852)

Considered to be the world's first programmer, Ada Lovelace worked with Charles Babbage, the inventor of the Difference Engine and Analytical Engine—an early mechanical calculator and computer. Lady Lovelace translated an Italian memoir on the Analytical Engine, and added a set of notes that describe how to set up the device to follow an algorithm to calculate Bernoulli numbers. That algorithm is considered to be the first computer program.

Lady Lovelace was the daughter of the famous poet Lord Byron and was acquainted with other luminaries of the period, including Michael Faraday and Charles Dickens. She received tutoring from mathematician Augustus De Morgan, discoverer of De Morgan's Laws, which have critically important applications in Boolean algebra.

3.0   INTRODUCTION

Programming is the art of writing software instructions that the computer must follow to accomplish some task. This activity requires a specialized knowledge of the programming language to be used, and is part art, part craft, and part skill, all of which take time and effort to develop. Efforts are underway to make programming more of an engineering discipline, which would make the process less creative but more reliable. Still, at the present level, programming requires experience, insight, and creativity. The process of programming is central to understanding what the computer does in following a program, and therefore also is central to understanding computer science and other computing disciplines. The importance of programming to different computing disciplines varies. Programming is less important for other related computing disciplines like information systems, where mere knowledge of programming and software design is needed, but not at the expert level. Not all computer-related careers will require a high level of expertise in this area, but computer science does require the development of a sophisticated and mature skill set in programming and software design. This text includes an overview of fundamental programming concepts, but is *not* intended to teach programming to the beginner.

3.1 PROGRAMMING LOGIC STRUCTURES

There are three fundamental programming logic structures, but with variations and seemingly infinite ways to combine these elemental logic structures.

1. **Sequence:** Simply the idea of executing instructions in order, starting with the first instruction. This simple concept is actually implemented in the CPU's hardware, which is set to bring in the next instruction after the current one.
2. **Selection:** Choices between alternative instructions and groups of instructions are implemented with IF statements. The IF statement will check or test some condition to see if it is currently true, and then execute one or another blocks of programming statements. The logic is:

IF [some condition is true]
   THEN do something
   ELSE do something else

IF statements can be connected together in order to make more complex logic structures. Specialized forms of IF statements have been developed to replace often-used structures with multiple IF statements. These are often called CASE or SWITCH statements and are designed for use when there are more than just two alternatives (THEN do something, ELSE do something else).

3. **Iteration:** Repetition or repeating a set of instructions is called *iteration*. Much of the power of computing comes from the ability to repetitively execute simple instructions many times very quickly, thereby accomplishing significant work. Iteration is also called *looping*. Iteration is implemented with two general types of statements:

WHILE [some condition remains true]
   Some set of statements

An alternative structure changes where the testing of the condition is located relative to the repeated statements:

REPEAT
   Some set of statements
   UNTIL [some condition becomes true]

These fundamental logic structures have been utilized since the dawn of computing with little change in concept, but with minor changes in naming conventions and specific implementation details.

3.2   PSEUDOCODE AND FLOWCHARTS

Pseudocode is the idea of using English-like statements to represent actual programming statements. Sometimes it is easier to think out a problem in English, and then later translate the solution into programming language statements (code). The concept of separating the design of a program from the writing of programming statements simplifies the complexity of programming (and learning programming in particular). This approach relies on the time-honored "divide-and-conquer" strategy to make complex problems easier by dividing the problem into separate pieces.

Flowcharts are an old but still useful technique for illustrating the flow of control (sequence of execution of instructions) in a program or inside a program module. This technique is still used and applied in a variety of settings and in teaching basic programming logic. Flowcharting has been supplanted by other diagramming and documenting tools for illustrating and documenting the construction of large-scale software design projects, particularly those created in uniform modeling language (UML, described in Section 5.6). Flowcharts even have found application in areas outside of computing and they are part of the common foundations of computing.

The three fundamental programming logic structures will be illustrated in both pseudocode and with flowchart examples:

1. **Sequence:** A simple rectangle is used to represent a group of instructions that are to be executed in sequence to perform some function. The flow of control is into the block, and then after completing the instructions grouped within the block, it continues on to the next part of the program. Note that in Figure 3.1, there is but one entry point and one exit point.

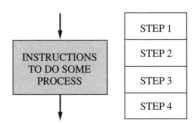

FIGURE 3.1   Sequence Flowchart and Pseudocode

2. **Selection:** A decision, selection, or IF statement has a diamond shape for the IF and the condition (Figure 3.2). Based on the evaluation of the condition (either true of false), one of the other of the two blocks of code following the IF will be executed next. If the condition is true, the

THEN block will be executed. If the condition is evaluated as false, then the ELSE block will be executed.

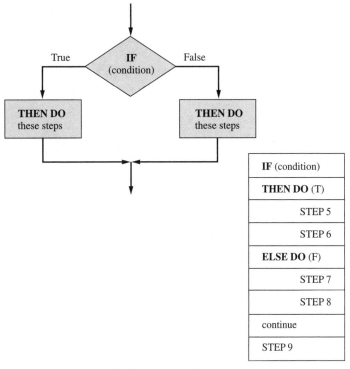

IF (condition)
THEN DO (T)
STEP 5
STEP 6
ELSE DO (F)
STEP 7
STEP 8
continue
STEP 9

FIGURE 3.2   Selection and **IF** Flowchart and Pseudocode

3. **Compound IF:** A compound IF statement is represented with multiple diamond shapes. Notice that dependency: the IF with condition 2 is not even checked unless condition 1 turns out to be true. Therefore the block of code labeled "THEN DO Steps 1, 2" is executed ONLY if BOTH condition 1 AND condition 2 evaluate to true. Also, observe in Figure 3.3 how the flow-of-control comes together after the completion of the IF code: The block labeled "continue these steps" is executed regardless of any of the IF conditions.

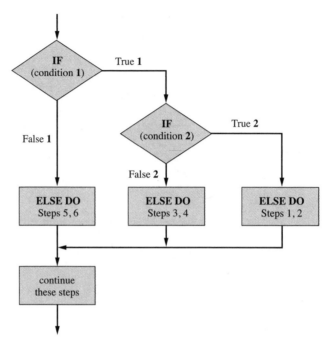

FIGURE 3.3 Compound **IF** Flowchart

The equivalent code for the compound IF flowchart shown in Figure 3.4 is actually pseudocode. It is not a real programming language.

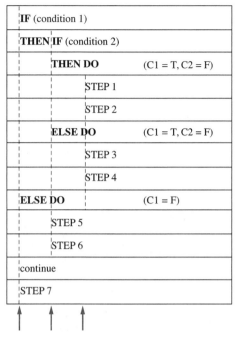

Indentation levels show logical dependence
on **IF** conditions

FIGURE 3.4   Compound-**IF** Pseudocode

4. **Iteration:** Repeating blocks of code in a loop are represented with the six-sided symbol shown in Figure 3.5. The figure shows a WHILE loop that includes a condition. As long as the condition is true, the block labeled "Repeated Body of Loop" is executed. After each execution of the body of the loop, the WHILE condition is tested again. The loop repeats until the WHILE condition is evaluated to be false, at which point the program execution continues with the rest of the program.

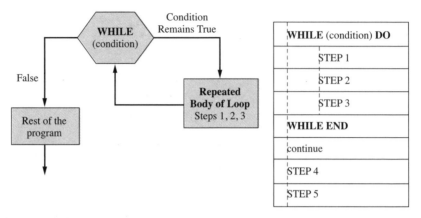

FIGURE 3.5 Iteration Flowchart and Pseudocode

3.3 DATA AND VARIABLES

The data and information used and manipulated by the program must be stored and accessed in some way. Programming languages allow the programmer to create VARIABLES, which store the data values while the program is running. The variables in a program are temporary (described as volatile memory) and exist only while the program is running. Data that must be preserved must be stored in a more permanent storage (nonvolatile), generally on disk, though nonvolatile memory "sticks" are becoming commonplace and are replacing disk storage for many uses.

Variables are named as such because the values that they store can vary, as the program manipulates and works with the data they contain. There are numerous TYPES of variables based on the data that they contain, depending on the specific programming language. Some common types include *integer, floating point, character,* and *string* (strings of characters, like a name, word, or sentence).

Figure 3.6 illustrates a complete simple program in pseudocode. The program has a beginning and end. Three variables are defined; the first two are of type integer. The third is of type float to handle floating point results from the division.

The data for each of the two variables is coded directly into the program. When Num1 and Num2 are created, they are assigned the values of 7 and 3, respectively. Directly coding data values into a program is a clumsy way to program; to make the program run with different data, the program itself must be revised. A better way (Figure 3.7) is to allow a program to obtain data from a user or data file. (Note that if Num2 was zero, the program will not function correctly since division by zero is undefined.)

The INPUT statement will allow the user to enter the data at the keyboard. It will display a prompt (the text between quotes) so that the user

PROGRAM Simple **BEGIN**
INTEGER Num1 = 7
INTEGER Num2 = 3
FLOAT Result
Result = Num1 / Num2
PRINT Result
END

FIGURE 3.6   Simple Program Pseudocode

PROGRAM Simple **BEGIN**
INTEGER Num1
INTEGER Num2
FLOAT Result
INPUT □Enter Number 1□, Num1
INPUT □Enter Number 2□, Num2
Result = Num1 / Num2
PRINT □TheResult is□, Result
END

FIGURE 3.7   Better Simple Program Pseudocode

understands what the program expects. Similarly, the `PRINT` statement will also print a description of what the number that appears on the screen means.

These simple programs look similar to an old programming language called BASIC (Beginners All-purpose Symbolic Instruction Code), an easy-to-learn language that is not used much at present because programming language design has moved into more sophisticated languages. Pseudocode can be even more abstract and less program-like than these examples, but should always be short, terse sentence fragments.

3.4   STRUCTURING PROGRAMS WITH MODULES

Computer programs can quickly grow in size to exceed the ability of the human mind to grasp in entirety at one moment. Using the divide-and-conquer strategy, we break large programs down into smaller pieces, where each piece may be simple enough to design and implement easily and reliably. This mechanism for dealing with complexity is critical to our ability to reliably design complex and sophisticated software in a reasonable amount of time.

The approach and process to building software in components and pieces has continued to evolve as our understanding of programming has grown, leading to new programming languages and new programming paradigms. Object-oriented programming is a relatively new approach, now widely accepted, which pushes the idea of construction by components (now called objects) to new, useful, and efficient levels.

It should be emphasized that the use of modules to structure a software program is for the convenience of the human programmer and is not an artifact of the digital computer itself. However, as software has grown in size and complexity, the need for programmers and software designers and developers who can work as a team has grown as well. The ability to break down a design into individual components that can be constructed in parts by different developers and then assembled into an integrated whole has been essential to the success of modern software application development. The process of architecting a software design focuses on the best way to structure a large software system consisting of components and on determining and specifying the ways that those software pieces will communicate and interact with each other.

Each programming language has its own syntax that directs how the programmer is to specify software components, modules, and objects. The general modularization concepts that have evolved will be presented in roughly their historical order of evolution.

3.5   MODULE, SUBROUTINE, PROCEDURE

This technique groups programming statements or lines of code into defined blocks called modules, subroutines, or procedures (depending on the programming language) with variations on implementation and details. Modern object-oriented languages group code statements into defined groups called *methods*. Each block of code or module (used here as a generic label for all variations of this concept) is identified with a name or label, which is a handle used in other parts of the program to call that module. The blocks of code that comprise the module or subroutine can be complex and may include many loops and IF statements. Transferring the CPU's attention from the statements in the module at the current location to the statements in a different module so that they can be executed is called a *procedure call*. After the CPU runs the statements in the module and has completed the instructions in the module, the flow of execution RETURNs from the module back to the original or previous location. A module may also CALL another module, so the design of the flow of program execution between modules may become very complex. Different programming languages use different keywords to define modules, subroutines, procedures, and methods.

Subroutine

Dividing programs into pieces or components is a fundamental technique that aids the management of the complexity of the overall program. Figure 3.8 illustrates a program execution that is interrupted with a CALL to a subroutine. Note that the CALL looks like a block of code to be executed (which it is), but with "caps" on each end.

The subroutine is then represented with its own flowchart, with a begin subroutine bubble and a return bubble, which are the starting and ending points of the subroutine. When the subroutine has been completed, the flow-of-control RETURNs from the subroutine back to the program that called it, where execution continues where it left off (Figure 3.9).

After the subroutine or module has been defined, it is sufficient to simply call the module by its name, and the flow of control will transfer to the instructions in that module.

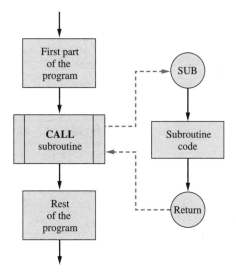

FIGURE 3.8   Subroutine CALL Flowchart

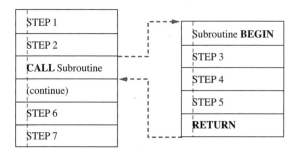

FIGURE 3.9 Subroutine CALL Pseudocode

Classic programming languages like COBOL, FORTRAN, BASIC, C, and PASCAL implemented versions of the preceding logic structures and concepts, while modern languages like Java and C++ add additional constructs to the toolbox.

3.6   PROGRAM EXAMPLES

Example I

Figure 3.10 illustrates a program that will calculate an average of three grades and display the average on the monitor screen. Each grade is stored as an integer and is assigned a value as part of the code itself. The three grades are first added together and the sum stored in **Sum**, then the average is obtained by dividing the sum by the number of grades.

```
PROGRAM Calc-Average BEGIN

    INTEGER Score-1 = 75

    INTEGER Score-2 = 92

    INTEGER Score-3 = 86

    INTEGER Sum

    FLOAT Average

    Sum = Score-1 + Score-2 + Score-3

    Average = Sum/3

    PRINT  "Average is", Average

END
```

FIGURE 3.10 Calculate the Average of Three Grades

PROGRAM Calc-Average **BEGIN**
INTEGER Score-1
INTEGER Score-2
INTEGER Score-3
INTEGER Sum
FLOAT Average
INPUT □Enter Score 1□, Score-1
INPUT □Enter Score 2□, Score-2
INPUT □Enter Score 3□, Score-3
Sum = Score-1 + Score-2 + Score-3
Average = Sum / 3
PRINT □Average is□,Average
END

FIGURE 3.11   A Better Average Grade Algorithm

Putting the data values directly into the program itself is called *hard coding* the data. In order to change hard-coded data, the program itself has to be modified, which is inconvenient and diminishes the usefulness and value of the program. A better program to calculate average grades allows the data to be input by the user at the keyboard (Figure 3.11). Now, the program can be run as many times as needed using different data entered by the user each time.

Notice that the score variables no longer have initial values assigned to them by the program. Instead, an INPUT command is used to prompt the user to enter each score. Each score then is stored in the score variables.

The revision and improvement of a program by creating new and improved versions is illustrated in Figure 3.10, evolving to Figure 3.11. This gradual improvement and development of a program in stages or steps is a common and natural way to develop a program. Section 3.7 elaborates on this software-design strategy.

3.7   THE SPIRAL OR EVOLUTIONARY MODEL

When programmers build software, the software designer repeats a design cycle that consists of only a few basic steps. This design cycle will be repeated many times as the project unfolds. The programmer will analyze a portion of the task, design a solution and strategy for this piece of the problem, code it in a programming language, and then test the project and design constructed so far. Any detected problems are fixed, and the designer then moves onto the next component and repeats the design cycle.

This section considers extending this common development cycle to a strategy for designing software. This "evolutionary" or "spiral model" consists of building successive, partially completed versions of a system, each one a building block or foundation for the next piece. Each version could be considered a prototype for the next version. This model of repeated building and testing one aspect of a problem at a time is particularly useful and helpful for the student; it will aid in minimizing the complexity of the task by making each step look easy, even when the entire project may appear very complex. This design approach is a great way to build confidence in your abilities as you develop expertise in programming.

The software design approach of this chapter is considered rather casual and informal, as compared to a more formal and tightly controlled process used in formal software-engineering methods.

When the Spiral Model Is Appropriate

Various approaches to developing software have been proposed, investigated, used, and adopted as standards. The evolutionary or spiral strategy is a tried-and-true approach that is particularly valuable for anyone building a software system in a new application area or with tools that are new to the programmer.

Other approaches to managing the process of developing software presume that there are few new technical problems that which will require research and the development of a unique solution. That is, most software-development methods concentrate on managing a process where discerning and developing the user's requirements and specifications is a primary problem, along with managing the complexity of a large software system with many components and multiple programmers or engineers working together.

This leads to the observation that there are fundamentally two different problem types in software development. The first assumes that the technical issues are solvable and known, while the structure of the software and management of the software-development process are the difficult challenges. Technically writing the code itself is not the challenge. The second problem type is when the issue of *how* to solve a problem using a programming language for a computer system is unknown or new to the programmer and that is the primary challenge. Then there are projects that will have a mix of problems in both categories; they are not mutually exclusive.

As a student of computer science, you are learning new problem-solving techniques, perhaps in new application domains, and perhaps with new programming languages, and so more often you are faced with primary challenges of the second type, with larger group projects that enter the domain of the first type. Professional programmers or software engineers with years of experience generally are faced only with problem types of the first domain.

When the *how* to solve a problem with computers and software is the issue—the process to be followed and overall structure of the resulting software—is generally *not* apparent at the beginning of the software-development cycle. The programmer does not have an experience base that can be used to project into the future how the work will progress. When this is the case, it is often useful to develop code using a cyclic model of analysis and development that "drills down" to a final product in repeated cycles of stages yielding ever-increasing complexity and completeness. Each preceding cycle of stages can be considered as the development of a prototype. The prototype is then used as the foundation that guides the development of the next level of system development and completeness.

This design approach is particularly useful in obtaining user requirements for a new system. When there is no existing software system to use as a comparison and basis for improvements, users who are not information-technology savvy often have difficulty in thinking about and defining how the application will be used in their work process. The development of a user-interface prototype is often a useful first iteration in the evolutionary design process, and in helping the eventual users understand and convey how the system should perform.

This approach may not always be as efficient as other software-engineering approaches. A system prototype developed at a given level will occasionally have to be significantly altered upon investigation of the details and complexity in the next deeper design. The redesign will make this approach inefficient compared to an approach that builds the entire system with knowledge about the system known beforehand. However, that is the problem: In new areas, with new tools, the critical foreknowledge of the future system and structure is missing.

This chapter develops a useful problem-solving approach for new domains and new tools. The presentation of formal accepted software-engineering techniques is left for courses dedicated to the study of formal software engineering.

The Spiral or Evolutionary Approach to Program Design

This software-design method has practitioners design software in iterative stages and possibly as separate components, with an eye toward building a completed project. The design and development process is broken down into the following phases, which are repeated in each cycle.

- **Analysis** of the requirements and problem to be solved
- **Design** of the next iterative refinement of the current prototype
- **Code**; i.e., writing the design in a programming language
- **Testing and debugging**; multiple iterations of testing, diagnosing problems, revising code, retesting

A project can evolve from a very simple structure (such as a shell or skeleton), where one piece at a time is added to the structure. Alternatively, the project could begin with a prototype-user interface and gradually evolve. This breaks down the complexity of a large project into smaller bites.

Often, in order to be able to implement/test/debug, each piece must be able stand alone, at least temporarily during this iteration of the cycle. The use of sections of "dummy" code as placeholders for later development is useful.

The evolution of the program pseudocode using the evolutionary software design method is illustrated in the evolution of Figure 3.7 to Figure 3.8 and also in the evolution of Figure 3.10 to Figure 3.11.

Before the creation by parts commences, an overall problem analysis and partial design is needed. The following version of the evolutionary or spiral model of software design differs somewhat from the originator's version:

1. Overall problem analysis
2. High-level design of a general skeleton or structure
3. Selection of a piece to work on
   - Analysis of one piece of the overall problem
   - Design for that one piece
   - Code
   - Test/debug
4. Back to selection of the next piece to work on and/or high-level design

As the implementation continues, it is possible that modifications to the overall design or project skeleton will be needed. This design philosophy assumes that high-level changes will be minimal; a complete redesign could be time consuming—if this method has a weakness, that is it.

The spiral or evolutionary model (Figure 3.12) of software development is perhaps the ancestor of "extreme programming" and "agile development," which are discussed in Chapter 6.

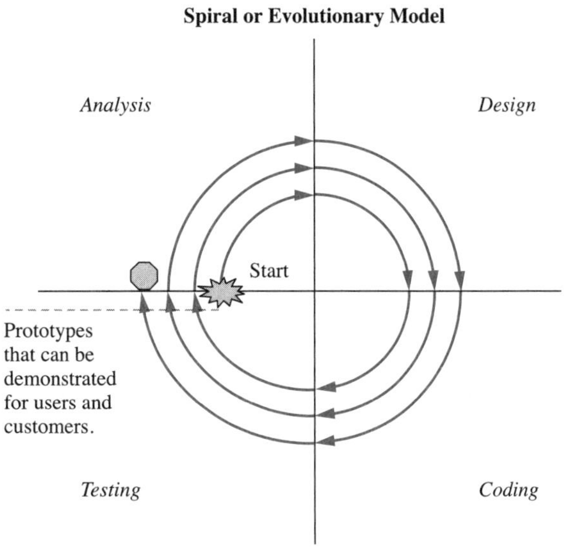

Spiral or Evolutionary Model

FIGURE 3.12   Spiral or Evolutionary Design Model

3.8   VARIABLES AND SCOPE

In addition to transferring the flow of control (the instructions that the CPU is currently executing) from the main program to a module and from module to module, data also may be transferred between program components. Each module can be defined to have its own set of local variables, whose contents may be manipulated within the module without affecting the rest of the program. This concept is extremely useful in building reliable software, because it allows the programmer to isolate different activities and processing, facilitating the divide-and-conquer strategy at which humans are adept. Not only can we divide the complexity of the flow of control between modules, but we can divide the use and interaction between data. This concept is called *scoping* and is implemented in varying ways in different programming languages. Details on how specific programming languages and families of programming languages handle these functions vary significantly and are covered in textbooks specific to each programming language. However, in order to implement this concept of isolating and restricting the "scope" at which data items can be viewed and manipulated, a method of transferring information between modules must be created in addition to the rules for restricting the scope of data and variables.

3.9   RECURSION

Recursion is a technique that can be used to solve some problems elegantly using repetitive procedure calls. Rather than calling different program modules, a module can call itself. Recursive modules and subroutines must be designed with some care in order to allow the program to eventually complete and not run forever, repetitively calling itself.

Recursion is a program-design strategy that utilizes a dynamic form of divide and conquer. The subdivision of work is not between program modules, which are statically defined in the construction of the program, but is between repetitive calls to the same module, essentially creating multiple nested copies of the same module.

One of the neat features of using recursion is the ability to have the number of recursive calls to the same module vary, depending on the data to be processed. For instance, a small data set may recursively call the same module three times (creating three "versions" of the module during execution), while a large data set may recursively call the same module 100 times. Thus the subdivision of work varies directly with the amount of data to be processed.

Recursion is a powerful but tricky program-design concept that is applicable to a substantial number of problems, but is not useful for all (or even most) program designs.

3.10   THREADED PROGRAMMING

Threaded programming, like recursion, is an advanced program-design mechanism that integrates dynamic behavior into a program design. The term "threaded" comes from the concept of "threads of execution," which describe different paths or sets of program statements that can be executed. Multithreaded programming includes multiple separate threads of execution, each in different program modules of functions that can execute independently of each other.

To explain the idea, consider a similar concept: Imagine building a software-application system that consists not of one, but multiple separate programs. Each program can be running in the operating system at the same time. The computer's CPU is actually switching back and forth very quickly between these running programs, so fast that on a human scale they all seem to be running at the same time. The separately executing programs work together to serve an overall function. Many commercial software systems work this way, including Microsoft's Windows operating system and Oracle's database system. These both consist of multiple executing programs (processes) running at the same time.

A multithreaded application uses multiple threads of execution inside the same program all working together as part of the application, rather than multiple programs working together. There are other technical differences and many interesting aspects of threaded programming.

Multithreaded programming is a software-system design approach that utilizes dynamic behavior to simplify the design of a system, rather than relying on a static breakdown of a program into modules and components. It is particularly useful in areas such as simulation, in which the software represents a model of some real-world system or activity. For instance, in a traffic simulation each automobile could be made to operate independently, with its own destination and driving characteristics, and could be represented as a separate thread in a multithreaded application.

Parallel processing can take advantage of multiple concurrent threads and execute each thread on its own processor. This produces faster overall performance, measured as *speedup,* and is considered in detail in Chapter 14.

3.11 OBJECT-ORIENTED PROGRAMMING

The development of *objects* and object-oriented programming is a relatively recent development and advance in computing programming. The idea grew out of the software-engineering concepts of the 1970s and 1980s. Scientists were learning that when dealing with software and hardware devices for storing and communicating data, it made sense to have one set of program modules for talking with each different device and to force all programs and components to work through those modules when accessing the device. In this way, a standard *interface* to the device or data structure was defined, which could then be used by any programmer and accessed by any module. By using a standard interface, errors when different implementations were defined from different modules are avoided. Device and data interfaces then become general and reusable.

The first conceptual objects took this basic software design idea and made it into formal mechanism. An object was defined as the data structure or device to be accessed, *and* the defined interface modules that access it, *and* local variables needed to exchange data and for temporary working use. In modern programming terminology, we call the interface modules or functions *methods*.

Scientists realized that this concept lead to other powerful higher-level programming concepts.

- Defining an object allows the idea of creating more than one copy of an object, each with a different label or handle for accessing.
- Similar objects that do the same thing but operate on different types of data can be organized into classes. This allows objects to be created from one source programming definition that can operate on different "things" (data, other objects, structures of various types).

- Classes can be designed in a hierarchy, where each class is a variation of a common parent type, and *inherits* various attributes from the common parent class, modified with specific unique attributes of its own.

These and other advanced programming concepts added a new level of power and sophistication to the toolbox of programming techniques, but not without a cost. Defining a program as a set of modules or components simplified the internal design of each component, but added another level of complexity: the architecture of the overall design of the modules. The power of object-oriented programming comes at a similar price; increased complexity in the relationships between objects, methods, classes, and inheritance between classes and derived classes.

Object-oriented programming in a specific language is beyond the scope of this book. Modern programming languages like Java, C++, and C# implement the object-oriented programming paradigm.

3.12 AGENTS

An *agent* is an advanced programming concept that combines threaded programming with object-oriented programming. Special objects can be defined as threaded, so that they may execute independently and simultaneously. The power and convenience of object-oriented programming is now available for building multithreaded applications, when the problem can be solved most easily with separate threads of execution or when the advanced power of parallel processing is needed.

CHAPTER 3 QUESTIONS

1. Why is breaking down a program into components (as in structured programming) helpful?
2. What does object-oriented programming allow the programmer to do that aids in building reliable software systems?
3. What is a programming language logic structure? List the three basic types.
4. Create a pseudocode program that inputs two numbers from the user at the keyboard, subtracts the second number from the first, and then outputs the result to the screen.
5. Create a flowchart for your pseudocode program of Question 4.
6. Create a flowchart for a program that will input a score from the user at the keyboard (an average between 0 and 100) and will output the letter grade to the monitor. Grades are at 10% breakpoints (90%, 80%, 70%, etc.).

7. Provide an example of a possible application where programming with agents leads to a good design, and explain specifically what aspects of agent programming make it a good design.

8. List and describe the four phases of the spiral design model.

9. Describe what can be learned from building a prototype.

10. When is the spiral design model of software development most appropriate?

Foundations of Digital Electronic Computers

C hapter 4 covers an introduction to the digital computer as a machine constructed from transistors and logic gates.

Prerequisite knowledge needed: An understanding of what a computer is and does (Chapter 2) and a basic understanding of the flow of electricity in a circuit.

4.0   INTRODUCTION

The simple logic of the computer must have an implementation at a very low level as the foundation of the computing machine. In the modern computer, this implementation relies on transistors. Very fast and efficient microscopically tiny transistors are used to build logic building blocks in hardware called *gates*. Just a few transistors are needed to implement the logical operations needed, and then these logic constructs (the gates) are used as building blocks to build more complex functions and ultimately the computer system itself.

Using the logic gates constructed from transistors, a reasoning process that relies on Boolean algebra can then be used to build the larger logic machines that can be combined to create an entire computing system.

4.1   IMPLEMENTING LOGIC WITH THE TRANSISTOR

A *transistor* is a simple electrical device that provides an important function; a control voltage applied as an input can control an output current. This allows small input voltages to be amplified to control larger voltages and currents. Transistors can also be used to construct feedback circuits where transistor outputs feed back in as inputs. Feedback circuits allow changes over time to be measured and controlled. The development of the transistor was one of the crucial technological developments of the 20th century, allowing tiny solid-state devices to be fabricated by the millions on a single tiny chip. Solid-state devices replaced vacuum tubes, which have a filament much like a lightbulb—and like a lightbulb, they burn out over time, resulting in an unreliable circuit.

Using the transistor as a switch is perhaps the transistor's simplest function (Figure 4.1). A control voltage applied to a transistor can enable the flow of current through a circuit. Note that the output voltage changes exactly with the control voltage. When a control voltage is present (a "1" in the table), a voltage at the output is detected. Essentially, the transistor is controlling the flow of electricity between the voltage source (V+) and the output.

The electricity controlling the transistor passes through a resistor (the jagged line) to complete the circuit at the ground at the bottom of the figure. The resistor is needed to limit the amount of current that can flow through the transistor because large currents can destroy small transistors. Similarly, there may be resistors in the circuit beyond the output (not shown in the figure) to limit the flow of current through that portion of the circuit.

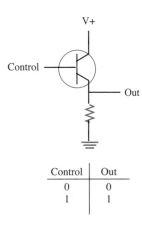

Control	Out
0	0
1	1

FIGURE 4.1 Transistor as a Switch

AND and OR Gates

The real power of the transistor is realized when more than one are used together to implement logic that is more complex. Figures 4.2 and 4.3 illustrate two arrangements using two transistors.

Figure 4.2 shows two transistors connected together in series. The series circuit forces the current to flow from the voltage source (V+) through both transistors (A and B) to reach the output and complete the circuit to ground.

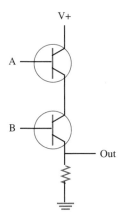

A	B	Out
0	0	0
0	1	0
1	0	0
1	1	1

FIGURE 4.2 AND Gate

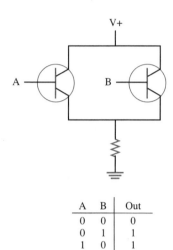

A	B	Out
0	0	0
0	1	1
1	0	1
1	1	1

FIGURE 4.3   OR Gate

The table below the circuit illustrates the logic that is implemented by the transistors. The output "sees" a voltage *only* when *both* of the transistors are activated. This circuit implements a logic operation called AND. The output voltage is present when inputs to A **AND** B are both present:

    OUT = A AND B

This circuit is called an AND gate.

Figure 4.3 shows two transistors connected together in parallel. Electricity can flow from the voltage source (V+) to ground through either of the transistors. The output "sees" a voltage when either input A **OR** B receives a voltage.

The table below the circuit shows that this arrangement of transistors implements a logical OR: The output is a 1 if either or both inputs are 1.

    Out = A OR B

This circuit builds an OR gate.

There are technical problems involved in this straightforward way to build an AND or OR gate, which will be discussed later. The following alternative construction also creates useful logic circuits.

NAND and NOR Gates

Figures 4.4 and 4.5 also show two transistors wired together in circuits, both series and parallel. Note the difference in the arrangements: The current-limiting resistor and the output have been moved "ahead" of the transistors (closer to the voltage source, V+).

Figure.4.4 shows two transistors connected together in series. The series circuit forces the current to flow from the voltage source (V+) through both transistors (A AND B) to reach the output and ground.

The table below the circuit illustrates the logic that is implemented by the transistors in series. The output always "sees" a voltage *except* when both of the transistors are activated.

This function is exactly opposite of that of the previous figure, because the output is located "ahead" of the transistors, close to the voltage source (V+). The only time the output does not see a voltage is when *both* transistors are turned on, creating an electrical pathway through each transistor from the voltage course to the ground. This alternative pathway through the transistors is low resistance, and the electricity prefers this easier pathway from source to ground. Essentially, the output value is shorted out.

The table of Figure 4.4 shows that this circuit implements a logic operation that is the exact opposite of the AND, and is called a NOT AND or

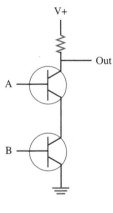

A	B	Out
0	0	1
0	1	1
1	0	1
1	1	0

FIGURE 4.4   NAND Gate

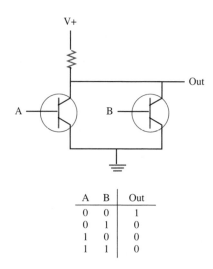

A	B	Out
0	0	1
0	1	0
1	0	0
1	1	0

FIGURE 4.5   NOR

NAND. The output voltage is always present except when inputs to both A AND B are present:

OUT = A NAND B

Figure 4.5 shows two transistors connected together in parallel with the output and resistor "ahead" of the transistors. Electricity can flow from the voltage source (V+) to ground through either of the transistors. The output "sees" a voltage when neither input A NOR B receives a voltage. If either transistor is turned on (it sees an enabling input voltage), it will create an alternative pathway between the voltage source and the ground. This essentially shorts the output so that it sees no significant voltage.

The table following the circuit shows that this arrangement of transistors implements the exact opposite of a logical OR, a NOT OR or NOR. The output is a 1 only when neither of the inputs are 1 and turned on.

OUT = A NOR B

The Transistor as an Inverter

A single transistor can create an inverter that reverses the inputs to make the outputs. The construction is simple and uses the same order of components as the NAND and NOR gates.

Electricity can flow from the voltage source (V+) to the ground through the transistor, but only when the enabling control voltage is applied. The

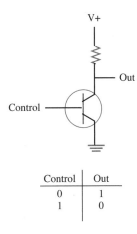

Control	Out
0	1
1	0

FIGURE 4.6 Transistor as an Inverter

output will "see" a voltage only when the control voltage is absent, because when the transistor is turned on (sees an input voltage), an alternative pathway between the voltage source and the ground is created. This shorts out the output by connecting it directly to the ground so that there is no voltage differential between the output and the ground.

Summary Table of Logic Gates

Figure 4.7 is a summary that shows a set of symbols for each of these logical operations and gates, along with an algebraic representation as a function and a truth table that illustrates the logic.

Transistors can be used to build AND, OR, NAND, NOR, and inverters. The inverter (NOT) circuit simply inverts or complements the input values to produce the opposite value as its output. It is a single transistor wired as a switch, but with the output and resistor located "ahead" of the transistor and close to the voltage source (V+).

In practice, there are technical reasons to prefer the use of NAND and NOR gates as opposed to AND, OR, and NOT gates. Manufacturing is simplified with NAND/NOR gates because either of those can be used to implement any other logic functions. The NAND and NOR gates are called a *complete set of operations*, because either the NAND or NOR can be used to build any of the other logic gates. Manufacturing a single gate type on an integrated circuit simplifies its construction, making it cheaper to build and produce. There is also a problem with the straightforward construction of the AND gate circuit as illustrated. A certain amount of control voltage will pass through the transistor, potentially generating a false logic. Some call this the *transistor bleed-through effect*. This problem is more pronounced

Name	Symbol	Function	Truth Table
AND	A, B	$F = AB$ or $F = A \bullet B$	A B | F 0 0 | 0 0 1 | 0 1 0 | 0 1 1 | 1
OR	A, B	$F = A + B$	A B | F 0 0 | 0 0 1 | 0 1 0 | 0 1 1 | 1
NOT	A	$F = \overline{A}$	B | F 0 | 1 1 | 0
NAND	A, B	$F = \overline{AB}$	A B | F 0 0 | 1 0 1 | 1 1 0 | 1 1 1 | 0
NOR	A, B	$F = \overline{A + B}$	A B | F 0 0 | 1 0 1 | 0 1 0 | 0 1 1 | 0

FIGURE 4.7   Logic Gates

if the gate is constructed with more inputs and transistors than just the two inputs and transistors illustrated in the figure.

William B. Schockley (1910–1989)

Schockley is best known for his work on the physics behind the solid-state transistor, which won him the Nobel Prize in physics (1956) along with colleagues John Bardeen and Walter H. Brattain from Bell Telephone Laboratories. The solid-state transistor is the fundamental innovation behind the growth in power, speed, reliability, and affordability of the modern computer.

4.2   BOOLEAN ALGEBRA

Conveniently, it turns out that there are easy ways to convert between AND/OR circuits and NAND/NOR circuits. One method is by using Boolean algebra. Boolean algebra is named after its discoverer, mathematician George Boole.

In Boolean algebra, a Boolean variable can be in just one of two possible states: it can be either 0 or 1. Boolean variables are represented with capital letters of the alphabet.

The AND operation is represented in a Boolean equation with the multiplication symbol (this is called *overloading* of the multiplication operator, giving it two or more possible meanings, depending on the context). The OR operation is represented with the addition symbol "+".

A **AND**ed with B can be represented as A · B (usually noted as AB).

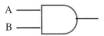

FIGURE 4.8   AND Symbol

A **OR**ed with B can be represented as A + B.

FIGURE 4.9   OR Symbol

Figures 4.10 and 4.11 show how the NAND and NOR gates are a complete set of operations. The circuit diagrams show how multiple NAND or NOR gates can be assembled together to build any of the other logic gates. Even though more gates are required using this method, in many applications the trade-off is positive by allowing the ability to manufacture a chip with a single gate type on the chip.

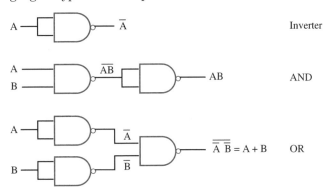

FIGURE 4.10   NAND as a Complete Set of Operations

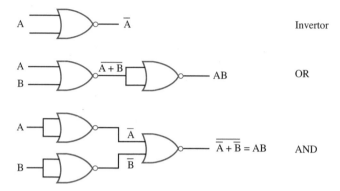

FIGURE 4.11   NOR as a Complete Set of Operations

Augustus De Morgan (1806–1871)

Mathematician and logician De Morgan worked to formalize the symbols and fundamental principles of algebra and the logic of mathematical induction. De Morgan's Laws are fundamental ideas in algebra and have specific application to Boolean algebra and the modern digital computer.

De Morgan's Laws allow the for the transformation between the boolean operations AND and OR, which allows the manipulation of Boolean functions to support their implementation in hardware with either NAND or NOR gates.

4.3   DE MORGAN'S THEOREM

One of the most useful principles in Boolean algebra is *De Morgan's theorem*. De Morgan's theorem provides an easy way to convert a circuit between AND gates and NOR gates and also converts conveniently between OR gates and NAND gates.

In the following algebraic equations, NOT terms or inverted terms are represented with a horizontal line over the terms:

$$\overline{AB} = \overline{A} + \overline{B}$$
$$\overline{A + B} = \overline{AB}$$

In the first equation, the left-hand term is a NOT AND or NAND of A and B. A NAND B is equivalent to the ORing of NOT A with NOT B. Similarly, the second line shows how a NOR gate (A NOR B) is equivalent to NOT A

TABLE 4.1 Perfect Induction Proof of De Morgan's Theorem

A	B	A AND B	A NAND B	$\bar{A}$	$\bar{B}$	$\bar{A}$ OR $\bar{B}$
0	0	0	1	1	1	1
0	1	0	1	1	0	1
1	0	0	1	0	1	1
1	1	1	0	0	0	0

ANDed with NOT B. Table 4.1 proves the equivalence through a process called *perfect induction*—listing the values for all combinations of 0 and 1—and by demonstrating that the outcomes are exactly equal demonstrates the equivalence of two terms. A single quotation mark (') can be used to indicate the complemented terms.

The columns of particular interest are the column for A NANDed with B (the fourth column) and the last column, A' OR B'. Reading the table from left to right shows how the last column is derived. By demonstrating that these two columns are exactly the same for all combinations of inputs A and B, a proof by perfect induction proves the validity of De Morgan's theorem.

De Morgan's theorem also provides a way to convert between OR gates and NAND gates; an OR can be converted to a NAND if the inputs are complemented:

$$A + B = \overline{\overline{A + B}} \text{ by double complement} = \overline{\overline{A}\,\overline{B}} \text{ by De Morgan's theorem}$$

In the same fashion, an AND can be converted to a NOR, if the inputs are complemented:

$$AB = \overline{\overline{AB}} \text{ by double complement} = \overline{\overline{A} + \overline{B}} \text{ by De Morgan's theorem}$$

The columns of particular interest in Table 4.2 are the column for A ORed with B (third column) and the last column, A' NAND B'. Reading the table from left to right shows how the last column is derived. Demonstrating that these two columns are exactly the same for all combinations of inputs A and B proves the validity of this technique for converting from NANDs to NORs and from NORs to NANDs.

TABLE 4.2   Another Use of De Morgan's Theorem

A	B	A OR B	$\bar{A}$	$\bar{B}$	$\bar{A}$ AND $\bar{B}$	$\bar{A}$ NAND $\bar{B}$
0	0	0	1	1	1	0
0	1	1	1	0	0	1
1	0	1	0	1	0	1
1	1	1	0	0	0	1

CHAPTER 4 QUESTIONS

1. List the advantages of NAND/NOR construction over AND/OR construction.

2. Draw a diagram using gates for the following functions:
  a. F = A + B
  b. F = AB
  c. F = A + BC
  d. F = (A + B)C

3. For the following circuit diagrams, give the equivalent Boolean function:

4. Prove by perfect induction, whether (A + B)C == A + (BC).

5. Prove by perfect induction this equivalence:

$$AB = \overline{\overline{AB}} \text{ by double complement} = \overline{\bar{A} + \bar{B}} \text{ by De Morgan's theorem}$$

Software and Programming Concepts

CHAPTER 5

Software Engineering

C hapter 5 introduces the important computing discipline of software engineering with an overview of the major areas in the discipline. **Prerequisite knowledge needed:** An understanding of what a computer is and does (Chapter 2) and what the programming process is about (Chapter 3).

5.0   INTRODUCTION

Software engineering (SE) involves the creation and maintenance of software applications by applying technologies and practices from computer science, project management, engineering, and other fields.

Software engineering, like traditional engineering disciplines, deals with issues of cost and reliability. Some software applications contain millions of lines of code that are expected to perform properly in the face of changing conditions, making them comparable in complexity to the most complex modern machines. For instance, the Boeing 777-200 has about 132,500 engineered and unique parts. When including rivets, bolts, and other fasteners, the airplane has more than 3 million physical components. The computing components in the aircraft dwarf the complexity of the physical machine with approximately 1400 processors executing 5 million lines of code.

5.1   THE NEED FOR SOFTWARE ENGINEERING

Software engineering is the study of how to use a defined process to create software. It turns out that developing software is difficult for humans: psychology tells us that we can hold in our minds seven different concepts at the same time, give or take a few. Software is much more complex than that; it is not possible to hold all the details of an entire program in our minds at the same time. This has serious consequences for our ability to develop correct programs in a reasonable time. Noted software engineering researcher Watts Humphrey notes, "Even experienced developers inject 100 or more defects per thousand lines of code." [1]

Our humanistic approach to this kind of problem is to use a divide-and-conquer strategy; to break down the problem into a set of manageable pieces. Then, each piece can be solved more easily as a separate construction, and the pieces assembled to make the whole. This concept of developing a program in pieces (functions, modules, objects, classes) has a drawback, though: It introduces new complexity in the interfaces and interactions between the separate components.

The software engineering problem is made more complex for large projects that require multiple concurrent software developers working as a team. Each developer must know how his or her component(s) are intended to integrate into the whole; the interfaces and interactions between compo-

---

[1]Humphrey, Watts. "Sweet Predictability." *Software Development*, February 2006.

nents must be defined and agreed upon by the developers. In this way, a software engineer will have confidence that the components he or she is responsible for developing will actually "fit" with the rest of the project and work properly in the completed software application.

Software engineering, then, is the management of complexity by following a defined process so that the decomposition of a problem into manageable pieces being engineered by different individuals will result in the assembly into a correctly working, quality solution. Software engineering deals with the communication and interactions between the software components, and the communication and interaction between a team of programmers developing the software solution.

Of particular importance in software engineering is reducing the number of "bugs" in the software, which are really errors or failure points. Perfecting a software product is the result of two aspects:

1. **The design of the software:** correctness, good design that supports testing and evolving requirements, and good design that makes implementation by a team of professionals an efficient process. Numerous design cases and models have been investigated and reported, leading toward standard practices that support the movement, making the software-development process an engineering activity.
2. **Human time and interactions:** the amount of time applied to testing and fixing implementation flaws results in fewer errors in the software. The interactions between individuals working on the project, and the division of the work between the programmers, can have a major impact on the degree of "finish" and reduction of flaws in the final product. In most computing systems, both hardware and software, human time is the largest component of system development costs.

The relationship between development time and product quality is illustrated in Figure 5.1. This figure shows that as additional time is invested in fixing flaws and correcting errors, the error rate naturally goes down.

An obvious question is, why do so many errors exist in the software in the first place? The answer to that question revolves around the inherent human limitation in dealing with complexity. The study of the human mind has revealed that people can deal with only a limited number of things at the same time. Because software programs consist of millions of lines of code, each with their own aspects of complexity, human designers inadvertently introduce errors and flaws when designing portions of the system separately. The separate software modules and components may not fit seamlessly together, requiring alteration and rewriting.

When a portion of code is modified or a new feature is added, the addition creates unintended side effects requiring more changes, alterations,

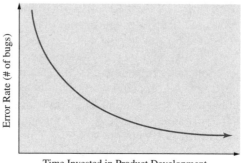

FIGURE 5.1   Ideal Curve of Time and Error Rate

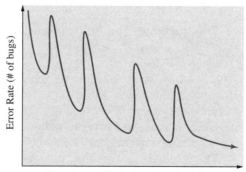

FIGURE 5.2   More Realistic Error-Rate Curve Showing the Effect of Major Revisions, Additions, and New Features

and fixes to accommodate the new features. Figure 5.1 is in fact an idealized curve, showing a smooth transition as more time is invested in the software development. In fact, an actual error-rate curve is jagged, where each addition or major revision creates a large number of unintended side-effect flaws and errors. Figure 5.2 illustrates a more accurate error-rate curve, with each up-tick in the error rate representing the addition of a major component or new feature.

The figure optimistically shows the error rate on an overall decline, with only temporary spikes in errors. The history of software development is littered with actual software development projects whose design were either too complex, required too many revisions and debugging, or were based on a flawed design, thus the error rate did not proceed down over time, but either leveled off or actually climbed. When a project reaches this point of crisis, either the project is abandoned due to lack of funding to correct all the problems in the design, or the time to complete the project exceeds the window of time beyond which the usefulness and competitive value of the project has expired. Sometimes the project is redesigned and started over by using only parts of the first design while accommodating the lessons learned from earlier failures. Software engineering as a discipline attempts to apply known processes and proven models to ensure that the development of software products proceeds toward a cost-effective completion, avoiding expensive and time-consuming mistakes.

A growing number of organizations implement process methodologies for developing software. Some of them are defense-industry related, because U.S. defense contracts often require compliance with specific development standards and processes. A short description of selected methodologies follows.

- One of the leading models is the capability maturity model (CMM). This approach utilizes independent assessments to evaluate organizations on how well they are developing software according to their own processes and standards. ISO 9000 describes standards for formally organizing processes with documentation.
- ISO 15504, also known as software process improvement capability determination (SPICE), models processes to manage, control, guide, and monitor software development. Like CMM, this model is about measuring what the software development group is actually doing during software development, with the goal of identifying weaknesses and ways to improve the process. SPICE also can identify strengths that can be continued or adopted into the common practice and organization's standards.
- Six sigma is a project management methodology that is being considered for use in software development. The methodology utilizes data and statistical analysis to measure actual performance, typically in manufacturing and service processes. Under six sigma, there is a maximum number of defects allowed, generally 3.4 per million per product or service opportunities. Because software development produces a much higher defect (error or bug) rate, and software development is not a repeatable process, six sigma would have to be adapted and modified to apply to software development.

5.2   EXTREME PROGRAMMING

There are numerous alternative approaches to developing software. One approach in favor for some applications is called extreme programming (XP). XP shares ideas in common with the evolutionary or spiral design process, rather than the formal regulated set of steps involved with formal software engineering. XP focuses on producing and testing prototype solutions quickly, and extensive testing and communication with the end user. XP runs a greater risk of pursuing deadends and having to back up and rebuild as compared to traditional software engineering, but the costs of making a change to system requirements is much less than with the traditional software engineering approach, which starts with "frozen" specifications at the beginning.

Traditional software engineering assumes that the entire project can be correctly anticipated in the design stage, prior to actually writing code. In contrast, XP is more tolerate of unknowns and evolving ideas and goals and specifications. Some consider XP to be the same as what is now called *agile development.*

5.3   AGILE DEVELOPMENT

A related development process sharing similarities with the spiral design and the XP methods is called agile development. Agile methods use the spiral or evolutionary design approach as a way to minimize risk by developing software in short iterations, which typically last one to four weeks. Each iteration is like a miniature software project of its own, or is like building the next level of a prototype. Each iteration includes all the tasks of the design process for that the increment of new functionality: planning, requirements analysis, design, coding, testing, and documentation. Although an iteration may not add enough functionality to achieve project completion, an agile software project intends to be capable of releasing new software at the end of every iteration through the design cycle. At the end of each iteration, the team reevaluates project priorities.

Agile development emphasizes real-time communication between developers, preferably face-to-face, instead of written documentation. Generally, a team of developers is located together to facilitate communication; by colocating all the people necessary to finish the software, including designers, testers, technical writers, project managers, and customers, communication is immediate and effective, resulting in lowered development time with fewer misunderstandings.

Agile methods measure progress or success through the working software that is produced through each cycle. Compared to the formally defined and regulated processes, agile methods produce comparatively little documentation.

Clearly, there is a major philosophical divide within the software engineering discipline between advocates of very formally defined and regulated processes with huge documentation and process overheads and the thread of thinking that begins with the spiral or evolutionary design process, through XP, to agile development. There may be an emerging consensus that the formal philosophical approach is appropriate for extremely large software projects and for those that must have a high degree of documented reliability, while the agile methods approach is appropriate for smaller projects and for those where time is of the essence.

5.4 DESIGN PATTERNS

Software designers and engineers have begun an effort to develop standardized "best practices" for solving and structuring components that are common, general, and appear often. A design pattern is a best practice for implementing and structuring a particular portion of code, which has been proven to be a sound approach and implementation through extensive testing, use, and application in a variety of contexts. A great many design patterns have been recognized and documented, but this remains an area of continued study and development.

The identification of these recurring, similar problems in software design leads to an examination of alternative ways to implement and structure a solution. It is worth the time and effort to examine and analyze alternative solutions structures when the component has many uses. The demonstrably best way to solve the design problem is then considered a design pattern.

Design patterns are particularly appropriate for object-oriented designs and programming languages, where classes can be instantiated from a generalized design pattern, and then subclasses can be developed that inherit the general aspects of a design pattern with specific details for a particular application. This idea illustrates a powerful feature of object-oriented programming: a general solution and module structure can be shared and adapted for specific applications. Each programmer can take advantage of already proven techniques that can be easily adapted, so each programmer does not have to "reinvent the wheel."

This is an important aspect of software engineering—an attempt to make software design less of an art and more of an engineering discipline, with known best approaches to solving common problems. The study and classification of design patterns is slowly leading toward computer-designed software in which a computer can break down a problem into a set of design patterns and then assemble and instantiate them to correctly solve a software-design task.

5.5 PROCESS MEASUREMENT AND IMPROVEMENT

Another aspect of software engineering is the attention to the process of building software in an attempt to get a handle on what is a difficult and intuitive process. Building software is not like building a machine, because the complexity of a design and the difficulty of implementing a design in code is not always readily apparent.

Therefore, a variety of approaches have evolved that center on measuring the process of designing software (after the fact) and moving toward fine-tuning the process to yield better results. The goal is to design software in less time with greater reliability and high quality.

Capability Maturity Model Integrated (CMMI)

Capability Maturity Model Integrated (CMMI) defines a set of levels for an organization's processes; the higher the level, the more "mature" the process used in an organization is considered to be. For instance, the most basic management practices are considered to be level 2 and most standard software engineering practices are considered to be level 3. Level 4 is about process and product quality management. Level 5 is about optimizing processes and management of technology change.

The first step in applying the CMMI concept is to perform an assessment of organizational practices relative to the models at each level. An organization's practices do not have to match perfectly. Based on this comparison, a maturity level is assigned to the organization with a list of strengths and weakness relative to the model. The output of this assessment then is used to prioritize areas that can be improved. The idea is to improve practices at the lower maturity levels that are deficient and then move up in maturity levels as processes are improved.

Software Six Sigma

Six sigma focuses on improving the processes to achieve lower software development costs, faster development cycles, higher quality, and lower software maintenance costs. The approach focuses on statistically measuring the development of software products over time, and then applying statistical measures to the data to look for potential problem areas and areas for improvement.

The unique nature of building software, as compared to manufacturing processes, affects the success of this approach:

- Every software module is different and unique.
- Every software developer has varying skill levels and a familiarity with a different set of ideas and techniques.
- A defect hidden deep within a software system can cause catastrophic results that render the entire system useless. In a manufacturing system, a defect in the manufacturing process generally results in a lower quality level in the product.

These differences between software development and other manufacturing processes tend to render the conclusions of the statistical analysis to be less reliable, with more unexplained variations.

5.6 UNIFORM MODELING LANGUAGE (UML)

Unified modeling language (UML) is a set of graphical systems for modeling and designing software systems that focus on the design and construction of the overall software as a set of software components. The emphasis is not on the internal processing inside a module, object, or component, but on the relationships between components. UML is a relatively recent innovation, coevolving with object-oriented programming and integrating the object-oriented view.

UML is a unification of software engineering modeling concepts and techniques into a single modeling language. It amalgamates a variety of modeling views, tools, and approaches into a family of compatible graphical modeling tools.

This overview will look at some of the main types of graphical modeling systems that comprise the UML.

Use-Case Diagram

Use-case diagrams describe the interaction between the systems' users and the system. Use-case diagrams are a high-level view of the system and the functionality it delivers to the users. They describe what the system is intended to do, but not the technical details of how the system will operate. The main components of use-case diagrams are:

Actors: These can be human users of a system, or other computer systems that interact with the system.
Use Cases: These represent the functions or services that the system is to provide to the actors.

Figure 5.3 illustrates a computer system for creating, sending, and managing email within an organization.

This diagram documents the purpose and intent of the email system, who the users of the system are, and what functions they can expect the system to perform. In this diagram, the figures represent users of the system and administrators, but in general, agents or actors interact with the system, which, in addition to people, can include other software and hardware systems.

Email System

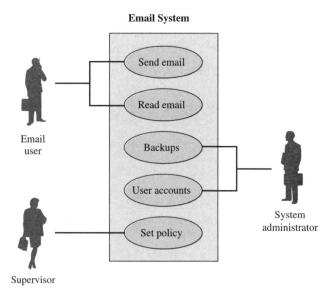

FIGURE 5.3   Use-Case Diagram for Email System

Class Diagrams

The class diagram shows the design of a system in terms of components that interact to fulfill the system's functions. In the object-oriented paradigm these components can be classes, and the classes can support interactions between objects using message passing and by objects invoking (calling) other objects. Class diagrams document the construction and organization of the software design through the design of the classes developed to create the system. The class diagrams for a system are tightly coupled to the features provided by the object-oriented software language that is being used to create the project.

Because subclasses are derived from and may extend parent classes, the class diagrams can show the interaction of the high-level class design, the hierarchical relationship between parent classes and subclasses, and the interactions between objects created from a class. A high-level class diagram may show classes and their relationships, but not the details of the construction or functions of the classes themselves. Figure 5.4 shows a simple use-case diagram.

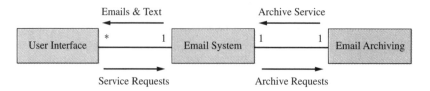

FIGURE 5.4   Simple Use-Class Diagram: Email System

In the diagram, the relationship between the user-interface class and the email system class is indicated between the two classes. The * and the 1 indicate that there can be many (*) user interface objects (one per user) that interact with a single email system. The relationship between the email system and the email archiving system is a one-to-one relationship. The transactions that pass between the classes also are described beneath the arrows going in both directions between the classes.

Another type of diagram is used to document and describe the relationships between classes and subclasses. Figure 5.5 shows how patient record classes might be organized for a medical application.

In this diagram, both the patient-account and medical-record classes are subclasses of the patient-record class. This means that they are specialized versions of the parent class. They inherit the structure and fields from the parent class, but also add additional fields unique to themselves. This ability to inherit from classes can be extremely powerful and specd application development. On the other hand, subclass definitions will no longer stand alone. To be understood, a subclass must be examined while also examining all parent classes. The object-oriented paradigm provides a number of powerful and useful features, but with the possibility for linkages and dependencies, many of these powerful features come at the cost of increased complexity from the human point of view.

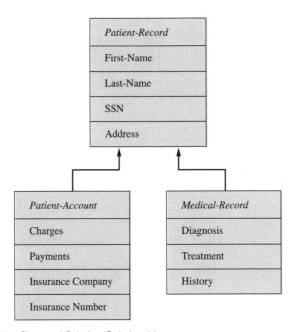

FIGURE 5.5   Class and Subclass Relationship

1. Explain the need for software engineering.
2. Describe the differences between the two primary philosophies toward software engineering.
3. List two software development process measurement standards.
4. When would agile development methods be useful?
5. Explain how design patterns contribute to the development of software engineering.
6. Briefly explain the differences in approach to improving the software development processes of CMMI and six sigma.
7. Search the Web for a software development case study in which the project was either redesigned with a clean start or abandoned.

CHAPTER 6

Elementary Data Structures

C hapter 6 is an introduction to the elementary data structures. Data structures are techniques for storing, organizing, and retrieving data, stored either in the computer's memory or on secondary storage (disk). **Prerequisite knowledge needed:** Chapter 5 and its prerequisites.

6.0 INTRODUCTION

Data structures are techniques and strategies for organizing, storing, and accessing data that is stored in a computer system. This knowledge area is technical with a theoretical flavor. Attention to efficiency, correct functioning, modifiability, and scalability are considerations in building and using data structures.

An understanding of data structures and how they are actually implemented in the modern computer is critical knowledge needed to understand how computers work, which every computing student should have. Data structures influence and are connected with other fields: database systems, distributed systems, efficiency systems, and algorithm analysis.

6.1 DATA STRUCTURES

Data structures are used to store and access data in an efficient manner, both in terms of time required to access and manipulate data, and in the space required to store information. Some structures are used to manage data stored in the computer's memory, while others are used to manage data stored on secondary storage such as disks.

The concept has evolved over time from the initial concept. Figure 6.1 shows a single data structure being accessed by multiple programs.

In this design concept, each program or application must incorporate the program code required to properly access the data structure. This is now considered to be extremely poor software design; a change to the code that manages the structure must be distributed to every program that utilizes that data structure. If one of the programs operates incorrectly, it could potentially corrupt the data structure for all programs.

Multiple programs attempting to access the data simultaneously can cause problems that corrupt the data. Consider as an example what would happen if one program was attempting to modify a piece of data, while at the same time another program was attempting to delete the same piece of data. Software techniques have been created to protect data from inadvertent

FIGURE 6.1 Multiple Programs Accessing Data

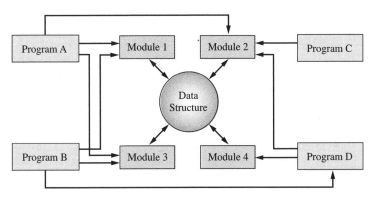

FIGURE 6.2 Access through Modules

corruption due to access from multiple programs and processes running at the same time.

Figure 6.2 shows the next step in the conceptual evolution of accessing data structures. It shows a set of common interface modules that are used to access the data structure. Each program must incorporate the modules that it needs to perform operations on the data structure. This could be done through building a library of modules that can be incorporated into a program by linking the library modules into a program.

The next step in this conceptual evolution is to make the interface modules sharable, so only one set of modules need to be loaded into the computer's memory at a time, and all programs can access those modules. Figure 6.3 shows that the modules are designed to be accessed by multiple programs without causing problems.

This concept saves memory, but also provides a simple upgrade path. If the access modules need to be upgraded, a new set of modules needs to be loaded into memory, replacing the old modules, and all programs that access the data structure then will be automatically updated as well.

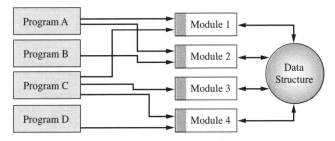

FIGURE 6.3 Sharable Modules as Interface to the Data Structure

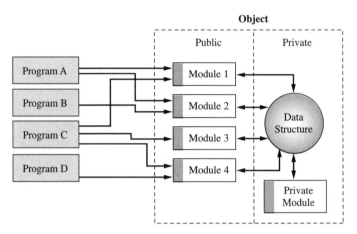

FIGURE 6.4 Object-Oriented Data Structure

The modern approach takes this design concept one step further, result-ing in the object concept. Here, the data structure and the program modules and code needed to properly access it are combined. That combination is called an *object* and is illustrated in Figure 6.4. A programmer can create multiple copies of the object (data structure + code).

6.2 ARRAY

The *array* is a simple data structure used for storing information while it is in the computer's memory. The simplest form of an array is a single-dimension table or a row of data items (Figure 6.5).

All items in the array are located relative to the first item. If the first item is at location "i," the other storage locations can be located relative to the first location.

Figure 6.6 shows that the array can also be shown vertically.

The array index is related to an actual machine address, as shown in binary in Figure 6.7.

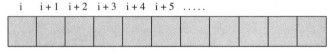

i = location of initial storage location

FIGURE 6.5 Array Access

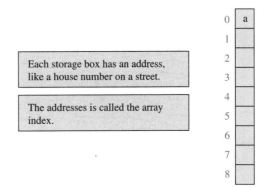

FIGURE 6.6   One-Dimension Array

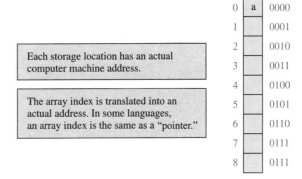

FIGURE 6.7   Array and Machine Address

Arrays can be used very efficiently in conjunction with loops. In the example of Figure 6.8, a variable **I** is used to "step through" the array, examining each item stored in the array.

Storage for an array can be allocated statically at compile time, which means that the location of the array is fixed and will always be created at the same location—or the location of the array can be allocated dynamically, which allows the computer to fix the location of the array in memory at run time. Dynamic allocation allows the array to be located flexibly in memory, so that the system can manage its memory resource most efficiently. The determination of how the storage space is allocated for an array is dependent on the programming language.

Figure 6.9 shows the array starting at a location other than "0000"; in this case at "1000." The array index is considered to be an offset from the

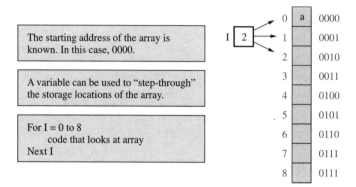

FIGURE 6.8   Arrays and Iteration

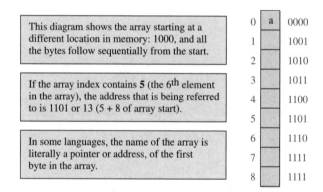

FIGURE 6.9   Array Indexing

starting location of the array. Therefore, every access to the array involves a small computation; the starting location of the array is added with the value of the index to create the actual address of the location in memory (sometimes called the *effective address*).

In Figure 6.8, a FOR loop was used to illustrate how arrays can be access in sequence, beginning with the first item in the array and stepping through each item. Arrays are stored in the computer system's main memory, which is *random access memory (RAM)*. RAM can be accessed in any order (including random order, hence the name).

Figure 6.10 illustrates this idea with a FOR loop accessing the array in reverse order while stepping by twos.

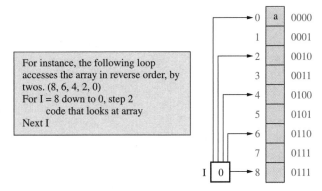

FIGURE 6.10 Array Access in Reverse Order

6.3 TWO-DIMENSION ARRAYS

A single-dimension array is a column or row of data storage locations, while a two-dimension array creates a table or matrix of storage locations. Accessing individual locations remains a matter of adding an index to a starting or "base" location for the array, but in the case of a two-dimension array, there are two indices: one for the row and one for the column.

Figure 6.11 illustrates a two-dimension array of 8-by-8 locations (64 storage locations), accessed with both a row and a column index. The highlighted location is (3, 6), which is in the row labeled 3 and the column labeled 6.

Note that because both the row and column indices start at 0, the row labeled 3 is actually the fourth row in the table, and the row labeled 6 is actually the seventh column in the table.

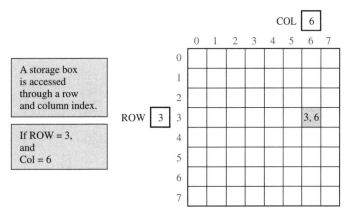

FIGURE 6.11 Two-Dimension Array

Tables can be accessed by the row and column indices, which generally are presented in (row, column) order. The reverse order is possible (column, row), but the programming language will specify whether (row, column) order or (column, row) order is used and it is important that the programmer be aware of the required method. Figure 6.12 illustrates that the same storage location is accessed by (6, 3) in (column, row) order.

As with single-dimension arrays, loops can be used to step through and access all of the items in an array. Having two array indices adds an extra complication. Figure 6.13 shows a code fragment that accesses all elements in a two-dimension array, proceeding by doing all items in a row and then stepping through the rows one at a time.

The example builds up the loop for accessing all of the items in a row first by using the column index. That loop is then nested inside another outer loop, which steps through the rows.

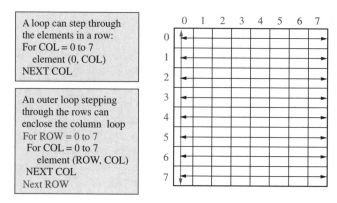

FIGURE 6.12 Two-Dimension Array Access

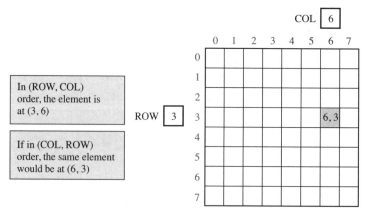

FIGURE 6.13 Two-Dimension Array and Loops

For each row, the column index will start over and go from 0 to 7, so that the inner column loop will run eight times, once for each row. The outer loop runs only one time.

In Figure 6.14 the addressing in binary of each element in the array is explored. Because this example is an 8-by-8 array with 64 elements, all powers of two, the addressing in binary works out cleanly. Three bits used to index the column, and three bits are used to index the row, since $2^3 = 8$.

The array can start at locations other than 00000000; for instance, the array might be located at 10000000 in binary (128 in decimal), and all of the cells are located as offsets from that starting location (Figure 6.15).

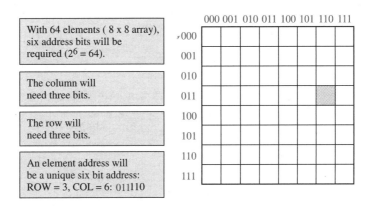

FIGURE 6.14   Two-Dimension Array Addressing

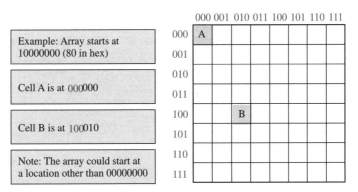

FIGURE 6.15   Two-Dimension Array Addressing Examples

6.4   ARRAY INTERFACE: OBJECT CONCEPT

This section develops a set of operations to work on an array. The array is viewed as an abstract data structure; as an example approach for later data structures that lead to the object-oriented paradigm. One might not actually access an array using this set of instructions, since languages provide more direct ways of getting at the data in arrays.

A set of interface modules will be considered for the array, to regularize access by multiple programs into the data structure. The following procedures (methods in OO terminology) will be developed to provide a standardized way to access the array data structure.

```
SET(ARRAY,ROW,COL)
WRITE(ARRAY,data)
READ(ARRAY,data)
INCROW(ARRAY)
INCCOL(ARRAY)
```

ROW and COL are private or internal variables specific to the data structure implementations and are not accessible except through these defined interface functions. Other modules must go through the public interface to the data structure to modify the current ROW or COL by using the SET, INCROW, and INCCOL functions. This allows the internal workings of the data structure to be hidden from the programmer working on other parts of the application. Hiding the internal workings prevents programmers from coupling their programs or modules to the internal workings of the data structure. This idea is called information hiding and is considered a foundation concept of good classic software engineering. (This example is intended as an instructional exercise and is not designed as a best practice or recommended approach for interfacing with an array.)

Figure 6.16 explains the SET operation, which requires parameters for the specific array (since there could be more than one) and the row and column. The SET operation will set the ROW and COL internal variables to the values passed as parameters, so that successive READ or WRITE operations will operate on the current location the array is SET to. The effect of a call to the SET function with parameters of ARRAY1 and ROW at 3 and COL at 6 is shown.

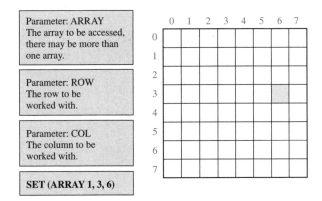

FIGURE 6.16 The SET Array Operation

The WRITE function can be used to store a value to the array, at a location already specified with a call to the SET function, as shown in Figure 6.17. In the following examples, the ARRAY1 is assumed to store integers.

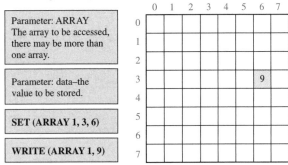

FIGURE 6.17 The WRITE Array Operation

The READ function will copy a value from the array into a variable that is specified as one of the parameters to the function. Figure 6.18 shows a call to the READ function to work with ARRAY1 and copy the value at the current location into a variable labeled TEMP.

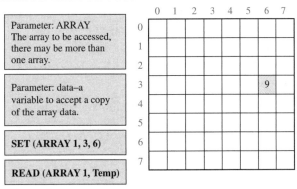

Temp = 9

FIGURE 6.18 The READ Array Operation

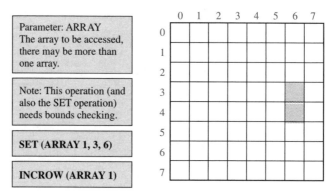

FIGURE 6.19   The INCROW Array Operation

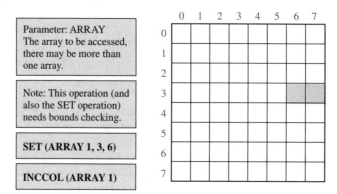

FIGURE 6.20   The INCCOL Array Operation

The function INCROW illustrated in Figure 6.19 is used to increment the ROW index to the next row. It takes as its parameter the array to be accessed. It changes the "current" location of the array by changing the internal index ROW.

Similarly, INCCOL will increment the internal column index (COL) to the next column in the array (Figure 6.20).

6.5   STACK

The *stack* is another simple data structure, one that is easy to implement and has only a few operations that are performed on it. A stack is a crucial component of the modern computer system, providing a place to store things temporarily and having a specific critical use as a place to store the current contents of registers and the program counter when calling a subroutine.

The stack is an area of memory, where one end is a fixed "bottom" of the stack, and the stack can "grow" at the other end (at the top). Items may be added and removed from the top only. Items not at the top cannot be directly accessed without first removing the items above it.

Figure 6.21 shows a stack with 10 storage locations. The bottom or base of the stack is at location 1000 and the current top is at 1003. This stack stores numbers; the only currently accessible value is 37, which is stored at the top of the stack.

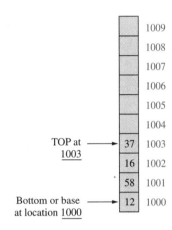

FIGURE 6.21   The Stack Data Structure

As data is added to the stack, it is added at the top of the stack. The TOP is adjusted to reflect the new top of the stack with the new data. Figure 6.22 shows that first the numbers 42 and then 81 have been added to the top of

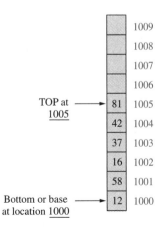

FIGURE 6.22   Adding at the Top of the Stack

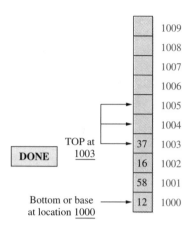

FIGURE 6.23   Deleting from the Top of the Stack

the stack. Note that as data is deleted, it is removed from the top of the stack, with the stack TOP adjusted to reflect the new TOP (Figure 6.23).

6.6   STACK OPERATIONS

The stack has two simple operations that are performed on it (besides creating and deleting stacks themselves). The PUSH operation places a new item on the stack and adjusts the TOP of the stack accordingly. The POP operation removes an item from the stack and adjusts the TOP of the stack toward the base.

PUSH (stack, value)

- Parameters are the specific stack (there could be more than one) and the value to be pushed and stored onto the stack.
- Checks to see if there is more available space remaining to add a new item and returns an indicator if the stack is full.
- Increases the TOP pointer to the next location in the stack.
- Writes the data value to the new stack TOP location.

Value = POP (stack)

- Parameter is the specific stack, and the function returns a value that can be assigned to a variable.
- Checks to see if the stack is empty and returns an indicator if it is.
- Decrements the value of TOP.
- Returns the value that is stored at TOP+1 (the old TOP value).

6.7 FILES

The file is another simple data structure, but this one is for storage on secondary storage (disk). There are both similarities and differences between a simple file and arrays.

Similarities

- Files can be viewed as an array, but they are stored on a disk rather than in memory.
- Each record in a file is similar to a row in an array.
- Each field in a record is similar to an array element.

Differences

- Fields can be of various types, while a simple array can consist of one type of item only.
- A file may store a structured data type, one that consists of multiple-data types grouped together.
- Nested structured types are allowed.

A structure is another preobject concept that allows a set of different data types to be grouped together (like a record in a file).

One of the uses for structures is to hold a record from a file while that specific record is being used by a program (created, modified, and examined). Not all languages support structures.

Nesting of structures is allowed; that is, a structure can contain other structured types. In Figure 6.25, STRUCT1 contains primitive data types, while STRUCT2 contains primitive types but also includes STRUCT1.

A record can be read-into/written-from a STRUCT conveniently because the struct elements match the fields of the records in the file (see Figure 6.26).

Figure 6.27 shows that an array of the structured type record1 can be declared.

In Figure 6.27, Array1 (of size 4) can hold the entire contents of "Employee File" with just four records.

```
Pseudocode:
Struct record1 {
        char;
        int;
        string;
        float;
}
```

Notice that record1 contains multiple data types.

FIGURE 6.24   Structured-Data Types

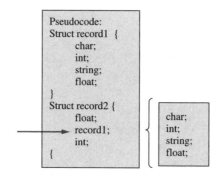

FIGURE 6.25 Nested Structures

Employee File

	Sex	Age	Name	Payrate
1	M	30	Joe	9.5
2	F	22	Sue	7.25
3	F	50	Mary	25.0
4	M	42	Mike	19.5

Struct record1 {
    char sex;
    int age;
    string name;
    float payrate;
}

FIGURE 6.26 Records and Structs

Employee File

	Sex	Age	Name	Payrate
1	M	30	Joe	9.5
2	F	22	Sue	7.25
3	F	50	Mary	25.0
4	M	42	Mike	19.5

Struct record1 {
    char sex;
    int age;
    string name;
    float payrate;
}

record1 Array1[4];

FIGURE 6.27 Arrays of Records

Elements in an array are static in size and fixed in type. This is because for most languages, the array memory storage space is allocated when the array is declared (Java is an exception). This preallocation means that the size of each array element must be known in advance and cannot vary.

1. Explain how the object concept evolved from a data structure with a defined interface set of modules.

2. Sketch a one-dimension array that can hold seven numbers. The array will be called "Numbers."

3. Duplicate your sketch from Question 2 and make the following stores into the array:

Numbers(1) = 5

Numbers(6) = 20

Numbers(3) = 5

Numbers(5) = Numbers(6) – Numbers(1)

4. Sketch a two-dimension array that can hold numbers called Stored-Nums. The array will be in (row, column) order with three rows and four columns, and will start out empty.

5. Duplicate your sketch from Question 4 and make the following stores into the array:

Stored-Nums(1, 1) = 7

Stored-Nums(3, 3) = 11

Stored-Nums(2, 4) = 23

Stored-Nums(1, 4) = Stored-Nums(2, 4) - 8

6. Define an interface for a simple stack data structure that is accessible from both ends (top and bottom). This double stack can grow in both directions from the middle of the stack. Your definition should be high level along the lines of Section 6.6.

7. Implement the two-dimension array data structure with the object-style interface functions described in Section 6.4, using pseudocode or a language specified by your instructor.

8. Sketch a diagram of Stack-1, that starts out as empty, and then the following operations are performed:

PUSH (Stack-1, 17)

PUSH (Stack-1, 5)

NUM1 = POP(Stack-1)

PUSH (Stack-1, 8)

9. Implement the stack data structure using pseudocode or a language specified by your instructor.

Complexity and Algorithm Analysis

C hapter 7 deals with the concept of complexity as it applies to computing systems, software systems, and programming. Complexity and algorithm analysis is a complex and theoretical area of study. This short section presents a brief introduction to the area. **Prerequisite knowledge needed:** In addition to an understanding of what a computer is and does (Chapter 2) and what the programming process is about (Chapters 3, 5, and 6), the student needs an understanding of mathematical concepts of exponentiation and logarithms.

7.0 Introduction

7.1 The Need for Analysis

7.2 Algorithm Growth

7.3 Complexity Analysis

7.0   INTRODUCTION

This section introduces an important and challenging area within computer science. Analyzing and exploring the behavior of programs and their efficiency is a complex and important aspect of computer science because of two issues: (1) poorly designed and inefficient algorithms and programs will waste computing time, and (2) some problems can take so much time that even the fastest computers ever made cannot solve the problems in a usable amount of time! Some problems and algorithms can require years of processing power, and that is definitely a good thing to know about a problem that one might be working on. The performance of algorithms and programs also is important when planning the amount of computing power needed as the size of the data grows.

A further interesting complication is that it turns out that some algorithms may perform quite well with small amounts of data but perform poorly with a large data set. So care must be taken when working with large quantities of data to choose the right approach.

7.1   THE NEED FOR ANALYSIS

It is useful to compare the performance of algorithms and computer architecture features as measured against the resources and operations required. This is so that a programmer or engineer will have some idea of the performance of the system prior to running it, the time to complete a certain size of problem, and the use of resources such as memory.

One might guess that most algorithms will scale in step with the size of the data set to be processed. Table 7.1 demonstrates this is not so; some algorithms are very sensitive to the size of the data set to be processed. For some algorithms the time required (and often memory needed) to solve a problem goes up dramatically as the problem size increases. At times it goes to the point where the requirements exceed the capabilities of the computer, or requires days, months, and even years to complete. Clearly, it would be useful to know if the algorithm being used is of this type.

Generally, we are interested in how the resources and steps/operations required grows as the number of data items involved grows. For instance, if we are searching through a list of items or records in a database, sorting the items or records, or building a multiprocessor system, we need to be able to quantify the behavior of the system as it grows in size. It is typical for data storage requirements of a system to grow significantly throughout the lifetime of the system; therefore the demands for computer system memory and processing time can dramatically increase.

Algorithms are analyzed to determine their dynamic behavior, and alternative algorithms and implementations can be compared to determine the best algorithm for a problem. This is a complex and demanding theoretical area of computer science, and this short chapter presents no more than a brief introduction to the general idea.

7.2 ALGORITHM GROWTH

This section introduces patterns of growth in work or resources required as the data set scales up. A modest growth is considered to be one in which the number of steps required to run an algorithm grows linearly with the growth of the number of items involved. More expensive algorithms or computer architectures have growth patterns that show an exponential growth in work or resources required, as the items involved grow linearly. A preferred solution might have the work or resources growing in line with the Log_2 of the number of data items involved.

For instance, the work required to process data might be described as a function. An example of a linear function is:

$$\text{Steps required} = 50 \times \text{number of items}$$

This relationship is called *linear* because if a graph of the steps required for data items were drawn, a straight line would be produced. The slope would be determined by the multiplier (in this example 100) on the number of data items.

Some algorithms perform much worse than linear. For exponential algorithms, the growth in work is related to the number of items as an exponent or power of some base:

$$\text{Steps required} = 2^{(\text{number of items})}$$

Often, it is most important to understand the magnitude of the growth in work or resources (whether it is linear, exponential, or logarithmic) rather than an exact equation or model that describes the growth perfectly. This is because for very large numbers of items (n), the details of the constants and modifiers are not the main determinants of performance. A notation is used, which represents the *order* of magnitude of the growth in work, and/or resources as the size grows, which is called "Big O" or **O**. For instance, an algorithm for which the work grows as the square of the number of items or elements (n) is noted as **O** n^2.

TABLE 7.1 Comparing Work of Two Functions

Linear = 100N Exponential = 2^N						
N	2	4	6	8	10	12	14
Linear	200	400	600	800	1000	1200	1400
Exp	4	16	64	256	1024	4096	16384

N	16	18	20	30
Linear	1600	1800	2000	3000
Exp	65536	262112	1,048,576	About 1 billion

Common growth models ranked in terms of the growth of work or resources required, as the number of items (N) grows from least to most (best to worst):

O logn   (logarithmic, generally log base 2 for computing)
O n   (linear)
O n logn (logarithmic)
O n^2 (polynomial)
O 2^n (exponential)

Figure 7.1 illustrates different orders of magnitude. In this graph, the number of resources required or steps required in an algorithm is the vertical axis, while the number of items (n) involved is the horizontal axis. Linear growth in work/resources is shown with a growth curve of **5n**, resulting in the only straight line on the graph.

The slowest growth in size (preferred), the logarithmic growth curve of **10log$_2$n**, is shown as a line that emerges at left with the lowest growth. For this growth pattern, the steps/resources required grows slowly as the number of items involved grows.

The steep exponential growth of **2^n** is the tallest line at the left, and illustrates an undesirable situation: where the work and resources required increase much more quickly than the number of items (**n**). Systems with these growth characteristics do not scale well.

Notice that the growth pattern that shows the most modest growth varies depending on the value of **n**. For larger values of **n**, the exponential curve is clearly the worst, but there are values for **n** where the exponential curve is the smallest amount of work (the lowest value). Knowing the order of an algorithm is important in understanding how its performance will change as the size of the problem scales up to larger values of **n**.

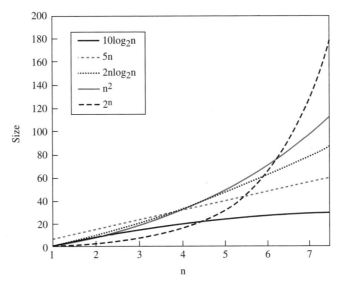

FIGURE 7.1   Different Orders of Algorithms

7.3   COMPLEXITY ANALYSIS

Complexity analysis analyzes problems, rather than algorithms, to solve problems. Problems are divided into two basic categories: those that can be solved in polynomial time and those that cannot. Problems that can be solved in $O n^k$ for some value of k are in the class called $\textbf{\textit{P}}$. These are sometimes called "easy" problems, and this class includes all those just listed. However, this class of "easy" problems includes those that require time $O n^{1000}$, which is clearly not easy to implement in the real world of finite resources.

All problems that are not known to be solvable in polynomial time are nondeterministic polynomial problems in class $\textbf{\textit{NP}}$. For these problems, there is no known algorithm to solve the problem in a definable amount of time. Consequently, NP problems are not candidates for typical computer processing and algorithms.

CHAPTER 7 QUESTIONS

1. Explain in your own words why it is important to understand the order ("O") of an algorithm.

2. Prepare a table along the lines of Figure 7.1 that compares the growth in work for a linear algorithm with that of a logarithmic algorithm. Recall that with logs, you must use a base. You might choose either base 2 or base 10.

3. Modify your answer to Question 2 to include both bases (2 and 10) in your table to compare the effect that different bases have on the results.

4. For the following algorithms and orders of magnitude, rank them in order of smallest size to largest size at different values for n (n = 10, 40, 100, 1000)

   a) $100n$
   b) $10n^2$
   c) $2n^3$
   d) 2^n

5. The factorial of n (designated as n!) is the product $n(n - 1)(n - 2)\ldots 1$. For instance, 4! is $4 \times 3 \times 2 \times 1 = 24$. Calculate the values of the factorials for n from 1 to 7, then compare the values for factorial against the different orders of Figure 7.1 and determine where factorial fits. Justify your answer.

PART THREE

Computer Systems Concepts

Machine Architecture

C hapter 8 covers an introduction to the internal design of a computer's central processing unit (CPU). The fetch/decode/execute cycle of instruction processing was described in Chapter 2. This chapter takes that concept further by explaining how that cycle is implemented in the computer hardware of the CPU. **Prerequisite knowledge needed:** An understanding of what a computer is and does (Chapter 2), the concepts of programming (Chapter 3), and the foundations of digital computers (Chapter 4).

8.0   INTRODUCTION

The internal design of the central processing unit (CPU) makes for a fascinating study for a couple of reasons:

1. The internal design of the CPU reflects the design of the machine language, to the point where the computer's low-level machine language is almost a specification for the design of the CPU itself. That is, when a designer decides what functions and operations the machine will perform at the low level, that design will require specific hardware capabilities. Making the desired low-level functions possible will require specific hardware and internal pathways. Therefore, the design of the machine language also specifies the hardware devices and pathways that will be required internally inside the CPU.

2. The second fascinating investigation is exploring enhancements to the basic computer architecture that have evolved over the years, which maximize the power and speed of the CPU.

8.1   BASIC CPU INTERNAL ARCHITECTURE

The CPU is traditionally described as having three primary components: a set of registers for storing values, an arithmetic logic unit (ALU) that can manipulate values (math and bit manipulations), and a control unit that controls the sequence of events inside the CPU and orchestrates the fetch/decode/execute cycle.

What needs to be added to this short list is an "interface" to the outside world; special registers for communicating data and addresses to the system bus, and internal buses for moving values inside the CPU itself.

The control unit won't be shown as a separate piece or component, because in actuality, it is arrayed on the CPU chip where it is needed, and where space is available. Figure 8.1 shows a simple arrangement of CPU components and shows that internal buses connect the set of registers to the ALU. Note that there is a cycle where values flow from the registers to the ALU, are processed in the ALU, and then flow back to registers. These components are constructed from gates and transistors that take inputs and create outputs.

The A Latch is needed because of the flow of voltage levels through the system. The A Latch is a separate register that is needed to hold a register value constant while it is an input to the ALU for processing. This is needed when the result of the ALU processing is intended to go back into, and replace, the contents of one of the source registers. Without the A Latch, the voltages would race through the ALU, through the registers, and then back again to the ALU, so the ALU would then see the resulting value appearing

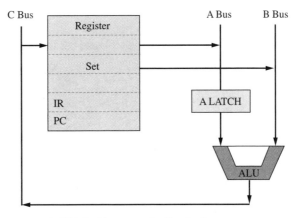

FIGURE 8.1   Internal CPU Architecture of a Simple Computer

as its input, causing further changes. To understand this fully, imagine if a register value contained the number 2, which is to be incremented by 1. Without the A Latch to hold the 2 constant, the 2 would be incremented by the ALU to 3, flow into the register and be stored as a 3, but also flow back to the ALU as a 3, to be incremented (again) to a 4, and back to the registers, and so forth. This creates an unwanted cycle and feedback loop. Therefore, in the case when a single register is both the source and the destination for the manipulated data value, the A Latch is necessary to break the feedback cycle. In the case where the result from the ALU operation is to be stored in a ***different*** register from the source, the A Latch is not necessary.

The job of the control unit is to set the correct registers to produce their outputs on one or the other of the buses going to the ALU, set the ALU to do the desired operation, and sets the correct register to receive a new value from the ALU. The control unit decodes the current instruction (based on the bits of the instruction itself) to determine the correct settings for all these devices and buses, and controls the sequence of operations.

8.2   CPU INTERFACE TO THE SYSTEM BUS

The CPU construction shown thus far does not have a way to communicate with the outside world (the system bus, memory, I/O devices, etc.). The CPU connects to the system bus, which contains bus lines for exchanging data and bus lines for specifying an address. The address lines are used both for specifying the addresses of instructions and the addresses of data. Similarly, the data lines are used both for moving instructions from memory to the CPU and for moving data between the memory and the CPU. A special register is needed for storing an address that connects directly to the bus address lines, and a special register is needed for storing data values that is connected directly to the bus data lines. Figure 8.2 illustrates these additions.

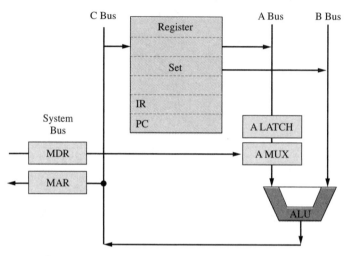

FIGURE 8.2 CPU Architecture with External Bus Interface

The MDR register is a memory data register, used for exchanging data and instructions between the CPU and memory (and possibly other devices). The MAR is a memory address register, used for specifying and address in memory to either read from or write to (and for communicating with other devices as well).

Consider what is to happen in the case where the contents of a register are to be added with a value stored in memory, with the result to be stored back into a different register in the CPU:

1. The first step is to move the address of the data value that is to be loaded from memory out to the bus. This address can be derived from a field in the instruction itself (details on how this is done are reserved for later study). The address flows from a special register called the *instruction register* (IR), which contains the current instruction to be processed. The address flows through the ALU (without being changed) to the MAR, where it appears on the system bus.
2. The memory is "watching" the bus and observes when a new address is posted to the address lines for it to work with. The memory internally processes the address and finds the values stored at the address.
3. The memory places the data values on the bus for the CPU to see.
4. The CPU latches on to the data on the bus, which is stored in the MDR within the CPU.
5. The MDR also connects through the A MUX to inputs to the ALU, so the ALU then can add the memory value from the MDR together with an-

other value stored in a register. The A MUX is a multiplexer that allows either the value from the MDR to flow into the ALU *or* it allows a value from a register to flow into the ALU. The A MUX, then, functions like a switch, allowing two possible inputs to that side of the ALU. The control unit circuitry determines what the proper switch setting should be for the A MUX, and controls the A MUX with a signal line.

6. The ALU then adds the value from memory on the A MUX input together with a value from a register on the other input side of the ALU to produce the desired result.

7. The result from the ALU then flows back along the bus to be stored in a different register in the register set.

What about the case where a data value from a register or being generated by the ALU is to be stored out to memory? The CPU internal diagram must be modified to add a multiplexer to the MDR, so that a value coming *from* the ALU can be stored into the MDR. The MDR must work both ways, both to store a value going from the CPU to memory and to store a value going from memory to the CPU.

Figure 8.3 illustrates the new connection from the ALU to the MDR. The MDR now has two possible sources of data, either from the bus (not shown) or from the output of the ALU. The MDR needs the ability to choose which source to take a value from, and will be integrated with a multiplexer to allow that choice, and will be controlled by the control unit logic and circuits.

The rest of the simple CPU internal wiring is logically determined by the required movement of data between the parts of the CPU and the system bus. The design of the processor instruction set (the set of instructions that the CPU must implement, which programmers use to control the machine) determines what the CPU must do; thus the design of the set of instructions

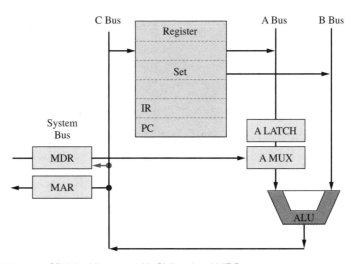

FIGURE 8.3 *CPU Architecture with Bidirectional MDR*

that are to be implemented generally precedes the design of the CPU internal architecture itself.

8.3 CPU ENHANCEMENT FOR INSTRUCTION FETCH

A special case for accessing the system bus exists when the CPU needs to fetch a new instruction. The *program counter* (PC) is a special register that is used to hold the address of the next instruction in the program. To fetch the next instruction, two things need to happen concurrently:

- The address of the next instruction (in the PC) must be placed in the MAR, so that memory will provide the next instruction to the CPU.
- The contents of the PC must be incremented, so that the PC will have the address of the next instruction to be executed (after the one being fetched concurrently).

The existing pathways can be used to increment the PC: Send the PC out on the A Bus through the A Latch to the ALU, where it is incremented, then out to the C Bus and back to the PC in the register set.

The PC must be placed into the MAR, and this must occur prior to being incremented. This means that the PC must also get to the MAR without going through the ALU. This requires an additional pathway in the CPU internal architecture (see Figure 8.4).

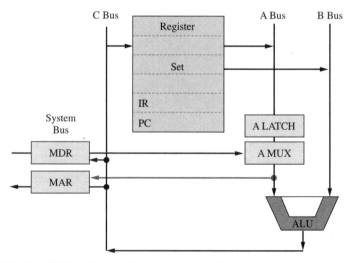

FIGURE 8.4   CPU Architecture Supporting Instruction Fetch

8.4 PERFORMANCE ENHANCEMENT: PIPELINE

The CPU construction illustrated to this point is consistent with the design of early electronic computers from the 1950s into the 1970s. In the modern computer CPU, a number of interesting, clever, and sophisticated performance-enhancing features have been added to this simple construction in order to achieve much higher performance from the CPU, as measured in the number of instructions processed in a unit of time. One such performance enhancement feature is the pipeline and another is the use of cache (covered in Chapter 9). The key to the pipeline is the observation that all instructions go through a similar set of stages while being processed (from Figure 2.4, repeated here as Figure 8.5).

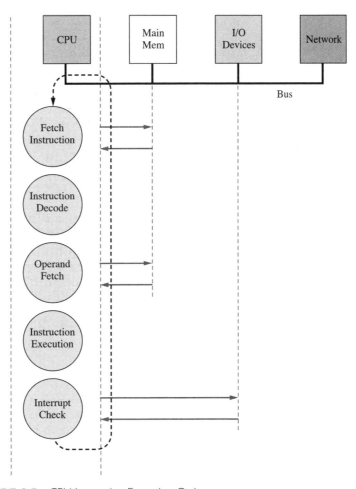

FIGURE 8.5 *CPU Instruction Execution Cycle*

The instruction execution cycle consists of five stages, the first four of which can create a pipeline inside the CPU:

1. Fetch the next instruction
2. Decode the instruction
3. Fetch any operands needed from memory
4. Execute the instruction
5. Check for interrupt signals

Each of these stages requires some hardware in the control unit or the ALU itself. When an instruction is being fetched, the other hardware used for the other stages is idle. Similarly, when the ALU is executing the desired operation, the other hardware components are waiting while that occurs. The key concept behind pipelined instruction execution is to run instructions through all stages of the pipeline simultaneously, so that all of the hardware stages are working rather than idle (Figure 8.6).

This produces a speed-up of processing due to the parallel execution of multiple instructions at the same time (though each instruction is in a different stage of execution).

Figure 8.7 shows a pipeline executing instructions over time. In the first cycle, the first instruction is fetched, and another instruction enters the pipeline in each successive cycle. The first instruction does not complete until after it has passed through all four pipeline stages, after cycle 4. This time delay between when the first instruction enters the pipeline and when the first instruction is complete is called the *pipeline load time*.

After the first instruction is completed, all remaining instructions complete in the next successive cycles, without this delay. The pipeline load time applies to the first instruction only. Once the pipeline has been loaded, the instructions are completed about four times faster. The speed-up in processing is roughly equal to the number of stages in the pipeline, in this case four.

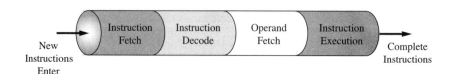

FIGURE 8.6 Four-Stage Pipeline

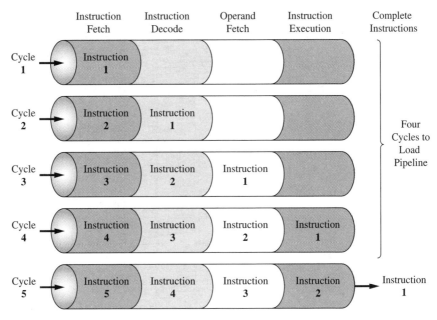

FIGURE 8.7   Instructions Flowing Through a Pipeline

8.5 MORE DETAILED PROGRAM EXECUTION

A more sophisticated version of executing the program than what was presented in Chapter 2 includes more details. Specifically, the program itself is also stored in the computer's memory, and each instruction must be fetched from memory into the CPU before it can be executed. The CPU has a special register that is used to store the current instruction being executed called the IR.

The computer's memory consists of a set of storage locations each with a unique address—like a postal address. These addresses are numbers, and each memory storage location is number sequentially. Names like Num1 and Num2 are associated with specific address: in Figure 8.8 Num1 is an alias for the location 00.

The CPU has another special register that is used to store the address of the next instruction to be executed called the program counter (PC). Each time an instruction or data value is needed from memory, the CPU must first send the address over the system's bus.

The initial state of the computer prior to executing the program is shown here. The program counter is set to the address of the first instruction of the program.

CPU		Memory	
Register	Contents	Location	Contents
IR		00: Num1	4
PC	04	01: Num2	5
		02: Result	
R1		03:	
R2		04:	Load R1 Num1
		05:	Load R2 Num2
		06:	ADR R1 R2
		07:	STOR R1 Result

FIGURE 8.8   Simple Computer: Initial State

The first step is to load the first instruction of the program from memory into the CPU's IR. At the same time that this is occurring, the PC is updated for the next instruction.

CPU		Memory	
Register	Contents	Location	Contents
IR	LOAD R1 Num1	00: Num1	4
PC	05	01: Num2	5
		02: Result	
R1		03:	
R2		04:	Load R1 Num1
		05:	Load R2 Num2
		06:	ADR R1 R2
		07:	STOR R1 Result

FIGURE 8.9   Simple Computer: First Instruction

Next, the first instruction is executed, which loads the number stored at location 00 (Num1) into Register 1.

CPU		Memory	
Register	Contents	Location	Contents
IR	LOAD R1 Num1	00: Num1	4
PC	**05**	01: Num2	5
		02: Result	
R1	4	03:	
R2		04:	Load R1 Num1
		05:	Load R2 Num2
		06:	ADR R1 R2
		07:	STOR R1 Result

FIGURE 8.10 Simple Computer: First Instruction Executed

After executing the first instruction, the CPU must fetch the second instruction (which is stored at location 05 in memory).

CPU		Memory	
Register	Contents	Location	Contents
IR	LOAD R2 Num2	00: Num1	4
PC	06	01: Num2	5
		02: Result	
R1	4	03:	
R2		04:	Load R1 Num1
		05:	Load R2 Num2
		06:	ADR R1 R2
		07:	STOR R1 Result

FIGURE 8.11 Simple Computer: Loading the Second Instruction

The second instruction is now executed by the computer.

CPU		Memory	
Register	Contents	Location	Contents
IR	LOAD R2 Num2	00: Num1	4
PC	**06**	01: Num2	5
		02: Result	
R1	4	03:	
R2	5	04:	Load R1 Num1
		05:	Load R2 Num2
		06:	ADR R1 R2
		07:	STOR R1 Result

FIGURE 8.12   Simple Computer: Second Instruction Executed

The program execution continues to completion. The next step is to load the next instruction that is to be executed. The remainder of this program walkthrough to completion is recommended as an exercise for the student.

CHAPTER 8 QUESTIONS

1. Explain the sequence and flow through the internal CPU that is required to store a data value from a register to a memory location.

2. Explain the sequence and flow through the internal CPU that is required to move a data value from a register into the CPU.

3. Explain the sequence and flow through the internal CPU that is required to add two operands (values stored in registers) together and store the result back into the register of one of the operands.

4. Explain the sequence and flow through the internal CPU that is required to add two operands (values stored in registers) together and store the result to a memory location.

5. What is the speed-up that could be obtained from a five-stage pipeline, disregarding the pipeline load time?

6. Consider the simple pipeline of Figure 8.6. Which stages in the pipeline access memory and which stages are completed entirely within the CPU itself?

7. The bus and memory can typically allow the CPU to access one value at a time in memory. If two pipeline stages both need to access memory at the same time, one stage or the other will have to wait (stall). Suggest a possible fix for this problem (called a *structural hazard*).

8. Complete the program walkthrough of Section 8.5.

Cache

Chapter 9 covers an introduction to the crucial technology of caching. Without caching, CPUs would run at the speed of the bus (one-sixth or slower speed), disk drives would be stuck in molasses, and the Internet would be so slow it would be almost unusable. **Prerequisite knowledge needed:** Chapter 8: Machine Architecture.

9.0 Introduction

9.1 The Need for Cache

9.2 Enhancing Performance with Cache

9.3 Fully Associative Cache

9.0   INTRODUCTION

Cache is an important technology that is used to improve many aspects of computing systems. The basic idea is to use a small amount of high-speed and local memory as temporary storage, in order to buffer the interaction with a slower device. The most needed data is kept in the fast cache, and the machine only has to look in the slower memory or on the slower device, when it needs something that is not in the cache. Cache can improve the performance of a computing system tremendously, as the frequency of a machine finding what it needs in cache can be extremely high (99 percent or more for some applications).

Cache can be applied across computing from the Internet and the World Wide Web to inside the CPU chip itself. All modern computer systems utilize cache in multiple places in the system.

9.1   THE NEED FOR CACHE

Historically, memory performance has not kept pace with processor performance, creating a **disparity** between two critical components of a computer system—or put another way, the cost in making memory perform at a certain level is much higher than the cost of making a processor that runs at that same speed. This disparity in performance potentially creates a *performance bottleneck* that limits the overall speed of a computer system to the speed of the memory system. In addition, the Von Neumann computer system architecture exacerbates this disparity by requiring multiple memory accesses for each instruction. In addition to fetching the instruction from memory, many instructions also require one or more operands that also come from memory along with the instruction. Figure 9.1 illustrates the Von Neumann bottleneck.

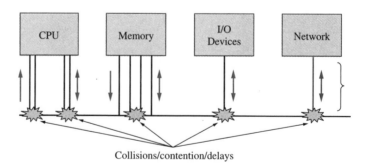

Collisions/contention/delays

FIGURE 9.1   Von Neumann Bottleneck

The use of pipelines as a technique that increases the number of instructions that can be completed in a given time period further multiplies this bottleneck problem. Increasing the number of instructions and operands that can be processed further increases the memory/bus bandwidth required to keep up with the demands of the processor. (Here, bandwidth is used in its common computing meaning—i.e., being the communication quantity measured in terms of bits per second, rather than its more traditional communications usage as a range of radio frequencies.)

Clearly, computer system performance has, in fact, continued to increase as the performance of processors also continues to increase, because computers continue to get more powerful and faster with each generation. This implies that there must, in fact, be a practical solution to this performance disparity, one that mitigates the performance bottleneck effects. That solution is caching.

Caching is a technique that reduces the data transfer demands of the processor that go over the bus to the memory. By holding the instructions and data values currently being used in a small, relatively expensive but very-high-speed memory called a *cache*, the CPU often will find the data that it is searching for in the cache. The cache is fast enough to keep up with the demands of high-speed processors, so accessing data and instructions in the cache does not slow down the processor. It is only when the processor requests access to memory that is *not* currently in the temporary high-speed cache, that a request for data or instructions must go out on the bus to the system memory. The idea is that most of the time, the processor can get what it needs from the high-speed cache, and only occasionally will it have to slow down to load a new block of data or instructions from memory into the cache. Following that loading of a block of data or instructions into the cache, the processor then can proceed again at high speed. Figure 9.2 shows a system with cache between the CPU and memory.

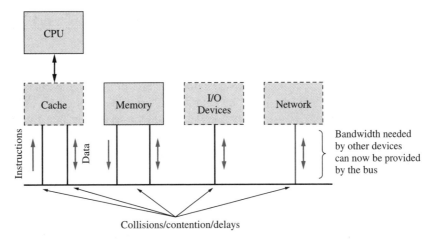

FIGURE 9.2 System with Cache

Caching is truly an effective mechanism that has turned out to be highly effective. It has been applied to a number of different problems in computing where a disparity in speed of access exists:

- Caching blocks of memory to solve the disparity between the performance of the CPU and memory. This cache is located on the processor side of the bus, so that memory requests that are satisfied by the cache do not need to use the bus, freeing that resource for other uses.
- Caching hard-drive data to mitigate the performance disparity between the hard drive and main memory.
- Caching blocks of memory that are in use by multiple processors in a multiprocessor or multicomputer parallel system; to mitigate the time to access (called *latency*) between memory that is local to one processor and is nonlocal to other processors, and which is accessed by distant processors at a higher latency than the access time from the local processor.
- Caching blocks of data in a multiple-processor system in order to reduce the bandwidth requirements on the interconnection network between the processors. Reducing the bandwidth requirements of the processors on the bus/memory system allows more processors to access a shared bus or interconnection network before the bandwidth demands overload the interconnection network bandwidth capability.
- Caching blocks of data in a communication system like the Internet, to mitigate the effects of communication latency for data (or web pages) that are held remote from the requesting processor, and to reduce the overall bandwidth demands on a system with hundreds, thousands, or millions of computers.
- Caching information about running programs in a multiple-user system, where the operating system must share the CPU between many users and between many running programs. Caching is used to reduce the amount of time required to switch from one running program (called a *process*) to another process. The switching is called a *context switch*, and this special-purpose cache for this purpose might be called a *register set* or *register file*.

It turns out that caching in practice is highly successful. Its universal and wide application to many different problems where there is a performance disparity or a need to reduce interconnect bandwidth leads to the description of cache as the *universal computing Band-Aid*.

It is worth considering the following principles behind caching and why caching works so well. The foundation observations behind caching are the locality principles. These have to do with the patterns of access in memory locations over time by the processor.

Temporal locality principle: The most recently accessed memory locations are more likely to be accessed again in the immediate future than are less-recently accessed memory locations.

Spatial locality principle: Blocks of memory that are near to the most-recently access memory block are more likely to be accessed in the future than are blocks that are farther away.

What characteristics of programs when they are being executed yield these observations?

- Programs contain loops that repeat the same instructions in the same areas of code (both locality principles). These loops may repeat anywhere from a handful of times to millions of times.
- Programs are sequential; the next instruction in orders is also the most likely to be needed (spatial locality).
- Data processing is often sequential; data may be organized in fields and records and may be accessed in the order that they are stored in the system.
- Memory is cached in blocks of size—anywhere from 0.5K to 2K bytes per block are common. The two locality principles imply that it makes sense to store the memory blocks that are most likely to be accessed memory in the future in expensive high-speed memory. This will yield a high probability that many accesses will be satisfied by the cache, yielding on average a faster memory response time.
- These two principles say that the most-recently accessed memory block is very likely to be accessed again, so it pays off to store it in the high-speed cache. Less likely to be accessed blocks will be stored in slower memory, and perhaps even on secondary storage (disk) in a virtual memory system. Some percentage of memory accesses will be satisfied very quickly (low latency) in the cache, while the remainder will require access to the slower memory. The average rate of access will be between the low-latency cache and the high-latency memory. The greater the percentage that can be handled by the cache, the lower the average memory access latency.

9.2 ENHANCING PERFORMANCE WITH CACHE

The computer system has memory storage components that respond at different speeds, building inherent performance disparities. A memory latency hierarchy exists in computer systems:

- cache
- memory
- hard disk
- networked storage
- backup tape storage

Cache improves the average performance of a system:

- The accesses or requests that are satisfied by the cache are termed *hits* in the cache. This fraction of memory accesses occurs at the speed of the fast cache.
- The accesses or requests that are not satisfied by the cache (have to go out to memory or other storage) are termed *cache misses*. This percentage of requests for memory/memory access occurs at the slower latency of the system memory.

All requests for memory are satisfied by either the cache or the system memory. This leads to a simple way to model the performance improvements that results from the use of cache.

$$Prop(hit) + Prob(miss) = 1$$

Average system request access performance then is:

$$Prob(hit) \times Time(cache) + (1 - Prob(hit)) - Time(miss)$$

An example [a millisecond is 10^{-3} seconds, and nanosecond is 10^{-9} seconds.]:

Cache access time = 5 nanoseconds
Memory access time = 50 nanoseconds
Cache hit rate = 90% (0.9)

$$
\begin{aligned}
\textbf{Average Latency} &= Probability(hit) \times Time(cache) \\
&\quad + (1 - Probability(hit)) \times Time(miss) \\
&= 0.9(5) + 0.1(50) \\
&= 4.5 + 5 = 9.5 \text{ ns}
\end{aligned}
$$

Observe that the average system latency with cache at 9.5ns is much better than the performance of the memory alone (50ns).

An obvious question is to wonder if high cache hit rates are reasonable for real-world applications. Experiments have demonstrated that the answer to this question is yes! In fact, in many cases, cache hit rates in the high 90 percent range are common.

Another question for exploration is the effect of cache hit rates on overall memory system performance. The following calculations explore the average latencies that result from varying cache hit rates:

Hit Rate

50%	$0.50(5) + 0.50(50) = 2.50 + 25 = 27.50$ ns
90%	$0.90(5) + 0.10(50) = 4.5 + 5 = 9.5$ ns
95%	$0.95(5) + 0.05(50) = 4.75 + 2.5 = 7.25$ ns
99%	$0.99(5) + 0.01(50) = 4.95 + 0.5 = 5.45$ ns

The effectiveness of caching also depends on the performance disparity between the speed of the cache and the speed of the memory. When there are large speed differences, there are large payoffs to using caching:

Cache access time = 5 ns, memory access time = 50 ns
Cache hit rate = 95% (0.95)
Average memory latency $0.95(5) + 0.05(50) = 4.75 + 2.5 = 7.25$ ns
Large disparity yields a speed improvement from 50 ns down to 7.25 ns, which equates to an 85.5% improvement
Cache access time = 5 ns, memory access time = 10 ns
Cache hit rate = 95% (0.95)
Average memory latency $0.95(5) + 0.05(10) = 4.75 + 0.5 = 5.25$ ns
Smaller disparity yields a speed improvement from 10 ns down to 5.25 ns, which equates to a 47.5% improvement

Other issues with caching must wait for future exploration in advanced courses:

- What about the effect of writing values to memory on cache performance?
- How to manage the blocks of memory in cache, to include moving memory between cache and system memory?
- How to search for and find the desired memory block in the cache? Because caching is intended to improve performance, the performance of the cache access itself is critical to overall performance.

Caveats to the above calculations, which are simple models:

- Memory speed is time to read a single value.
- What about blocks of memory? These take longer load times.
- Cache writes? Write to cache.

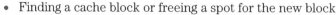

- Finding a cache block or freeing a spot for the new block
- The "miss penalty" could be much worse than our simplified analysis.

9.3 FULLY ASSOCIATIVE CACHE

This final section in this chapter covers an example of a fully associative cache. A fully associative cache allows blocks to be stored at any location inside the cache. This freedom to store blocks anywhere is very flexible and contributes to good performance, but the tradeoff is that the computer will have to check all the blocks in the cache to find the particular desired memory block. To simplify the searching process, part of the address of the memory block will be used as a tag in the cache to locate the desired cache block.

For example, a computer system has

128 MB (million bytes) of memory (2^{27} bytes)
1 MB of cache memory (2^{20} bytes)
1 KB cache and memory block size (2^{10} bytes)

From these specifics, information about the cache and memory can be deduced:

- The number of blocks in the cache = $2^{20}/2^{10} = 2^{10}$ = one thousand or 1 K blocks
- The fraction of memory that can be held in cache = 1 MB/128 MB = 0.78%

Because a block can be stored anywhere in the cache, a method of identifying the specific desired cache block is needed. In a fully associative cache, the memory address is divided into two fields: a *tag* to identify the block and an *offset* (or *internal block address*) to specify the location of the memory desired within the cache block itself. *All* of the cache block tags must be checked against the tag bits of the desired block of memory.

The necessity of comparing the tags for all cache blocks requires relatively expensive hardware to do quickly. The cost of this special comparison hardware grows quickly as the size of the cache grows. This cost issue constrains the fully associative method to be restricted to small caches. Other variations on cache design have been developed that trade off optimum performance for reduced cost.

Figure 9.3 illustrates the process of accessing a cache block from a 27-bit address using fully-associate cache. Because the cache block is 1 KB (2^{10}) in size, 10 bits in the address are required to locate the byte within the

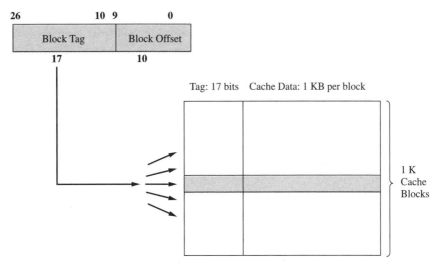

FIGURE 9.3 Fully Associative Cache

block (the block offset). The remaining bits of the address are used as the tag bits that uniquely identify each block and are used for the comparison.

The cache of Figure 9.3 requires a parallel comparison of tags of all 1,024 blocks that are in the cache, against the tag bits from the address. Requiring this many parallel comparisons requires a substantial hardware cost, making this large design an expensive fully associative cache.

CHAPTER 9 QUESTIONS

1. What is the purpose of caching in a computer system?

2. Explain why caching works well.

3. Calculate the average latency for a system with:

a. Cache access time = 2 nanoseconds

b. Memory access time = 50 nanoseconds

c. Cache hit rate = 98% (0.98)

4. Consider a computer system with a hard drive of 100 GB in size with an average access time of 20 ms (milliseconds). You are considering purchasing software to cache the disk using the computer's main memory. By using 200 megabytes of your machine's main memory, you expect to see hit rates to the memory used as disk cache of 95%. The latency for a cache hit (hit in the memory used to cache the disk) is 500 ns. Calculate the average latency time for disk access with the disk cache software. What percentage of improvement was achieved?

5. Where can a block be stored in a fully associative cache?

6. What is the primary disadvantage (that increases cost) of the fully associative cache organization?

Language Translation

C hapter 10 explains the process of translating programming languages to machine language. At the fundamental level, computers "understand" only numbers, and binary numbers at that. All other high-level representations of information must be translated into the simple binary representation system. A program that has been converted into binary code that the computer can run is called "machine code." **Prerequisite knowledge needed:** An understanding of basic programming (Chapter 3) and machine architecture (Chapter 8).

10.0   INTRODUCTION

Programming in machine code in zeros and ones is inherently hard for humans, because machine-code instructions are closely related to the internal design and construction of the processor itself. We prefer to use more human-friendly languages and high-level programming languages that are human-centric interfaces to communicate with our computing machines. At some point a translation must occur: to convert our instructions into a form that the computer can understand—primitive bits that can be either zero or one.

Fundamental to this concept is the shifting of work from the human to the computer with human-friendly interfaces that require more work on the machine's part, and less for the human programmer.

10.1   MACHINE CODE

A *machine code instruction* is composed of a set of fields (like a record in a database) for which each field has a specific use, and specific binary number codes in those fields represent different operations and events. For instance, Figure 10.1 illustrates a machine instruction format for a simple computer system. The numbers listed above the format are the number of bits allowed in each field. This instruction format has four fields, and the total number of bits in the instruction is 16.

The leftmost field (two bits in size) indicates the specific instruction format. The 00 in this field indicates that this is the layout for instructions of type 00. Because two bits are allowed for this field, there are four basic instruction types for this computer ($2^2 = 4$): type 00, type 01, type 10, and type 11.

Counting from the left, the second field is used to indicate the operation code or opcode. This is the specific operation that the computer is to perform, such as add, subtract, and the like. Because six bits are allowed for this field, there are ($2^6 = 64$) 64 different operations (instructions) possible in instruction format type 00.

The third field from the left is four bits in size, allowing 16 combinations. This field represents the operand that the instruction will work with.

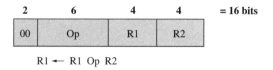

FIGURE 10.1   Simple Register–Register Instruction Format

Operands like registers and memory locations hold data values to be processed. For this type of instruction, the operands are all numbers stored in registers in the CPU, because the only operands allowed by the format are of type register. Any of the 16 registers could be listed in an instruction as either of the two operands. Other formats will allow operands that are stored in memory, which are referenced with an address. The fourth field is also a register operand.

The representation directly beneath the figure is a logical representation of what this instruction type does: It takes two operands stored in registers (R1 and R2) and combines/modifies them in some way as specified by the operation code, with the result then being stored back into the same register and replacing the first operand (R1).

Each field is stored as a binary (unsigned) value, so if the desired operation is to add the two operands together, the opcode must be represented or coded as the correct binary number. For instance, the six-bit opcode for adding two registers together might be 010000.

Specifying the operand registers is simple in binary:

Register 1 = 0001 (binary value of 1 in 4 bits)
Register 2 = 0010
Register 3 = 0011
Register 4 = 0100

Therefore, an entire 16-bit instruction to add the contents of two registers can be represented as bits for each of the four fields:

```
00 010000 0010 0100
```

From this set of bits, it is clear that this is an instruction of type 00, which allows two registers as its operands; that the operation is an add operation, and the two values to be added are stored in registers 2 and 4.

Machine-code instruction formats are actually closely tied to the internal design of the CPU itself. A specific CPU is designed to "understand" a specific machine code language, with definitions for instruction formats, opcodes, and the number of registers that are specific to this CPU. The hardware circuits that are able to "understand" a machine-code instruction are part of the CPU called the *decoder*. The decoder literally decodes the 0s and 1s in a machine-code instruction into the correct hardware-level actions needed to execute the instruction.

10.2 ASSEMBLY LANGUAGE

Working in binary is particularly difficult for humans, because it is tiresome and we are prone to making errors at this machine level. An easier language called *assembly language* was developed to make the programming process easier and more reliable. Assembly language itself did not add additional new capabilities or features to the machine or change its machine code. It simply substituted a more human-friendly set of symbols or acronyms to replace the raw machine-code bits. For instance,

```
ADR  R2  R4
```

is an assembly-language representation of the same machine-code instruction previously considered. ADR means to ADd two Registers together, while R2 and R4 are the registers that are to be added together. It is understood that for this particular instruction format (00), the result of the operation (in this case the sum) always replaces what was stored in the first operand. Other more complex formats might have a separate field for specifying where the result is to be stored. A program to translate assembly language into its proper machine code is called an *assembler*.

Later assembly languages began to evolve by offering improved features through a system of *macros*. Macros allow blocks or sections of often-repeated assembly code to be abstracted and represented with an placeholder abbreviation. The programmer could define a block of repeated instructions as "macro1:". Then in place of the block of code containing many instructions the programmer could simply write "macro1:". When translating the assembly language to machine code, the assembler will literally substitute the predefined block of instructions for each instance of the macro label, and then translate each instruction in that block.

10.3 HIGH-LEVEL LANGUAGES

Assembly language generates one-to-one machine-code instructions when translated: one machine code instruction for each assembly instruction. As computing evolved, the need for more powerful and higher-level programming languages that are easier to work with became apparent. In high-level programming languages, a single instruction might be used in place of a group of machine-language instructions that are often used together in the same repetitive pattern. For instance, the instruction

```
Sum = Number1 + Number2
```

might represent the four machine-language instructions to load the operands (Number1, Number2) from the computer's memory into two registers (two machine instructions), add them together (one machine instruction), and then store the result back to memory at the location called Sum (one machine instruction).

Languages like C, C++, Cobol, Fortran, and Pascal are all compiled languages, where the program that is run that does the translation of the high-level program instruction to machine code is called a *compiler*. The compiler will run through the set of instructions written in the high-level language and create a new machine-code program. The high-level program instructions cannot be run by the computer directly, but the new machine-code program that results from the translation by the compiler *can* be executed by the computer (Figure 10.2). This translation (compiling) need be done only once for a finished program and the machine-code program that results may be executed as many times as desired. However, if the high-level language program is modified, the program must then be recompiled to create a new executable machine-code program.

An alternative translation mechanism for high-level languages is called an *interpreter*. An interpreter does not produce a machine-code program to be run. Instead, the interpreter translates one high-level language instruction at a time and immediately passes that translated instruction to the processor to be executed (Figure 10.3). Interpreted computer languages are traditionally slower than compiled language programs because each instruction must be translated while the program is being run, and instructions that are repeated may have to be retranslated each time. Interpreted languages include BASIC and VisualBASIC.

A modern take on interpretation has evolved for the Java language and the Internet, where an interpreter/run-time environment is installed on each

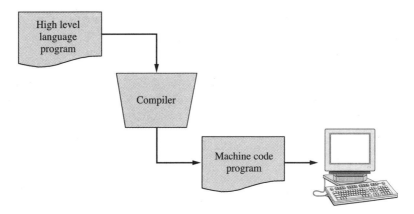

FIGURE 10.2 Compiling a Program

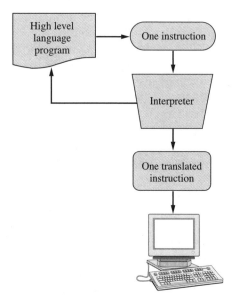

FIGURE 10.3   Interpreting a Program

computer that will run Java. The interpreter/run-time environment is specific to the processor and machine code that it will run on. Then, any Java program can be run on any machine anywhere, independent of the machine code and processor type. This run-anywhere flexibility is very powerful and useful and has contributed to Java's acceptance as a modern programming language.

10.4 BYTE CODE AND THE VIRTUAL MACHINE

An intermediate language translation concept has evolved that shares aspects of both a compiler and an interpreter. The goal is to improve performance over that of an interpreter, while creating a way to make programs more portable.

Each computer processor has its own machine code, which is unique to that processor family—yet we use many different types of processors in different computers, from mainframes to servers to personal computers (PCs) to personal digital assistants (PDAs) to embedded machines. To make a program written in some language portable to different CPU architectures, either an interpreter or a compiler must be developed specifically for that machine. Furthermore, the program must then be compiled using the compiler for that target CPU so the program can be run by that machine.

The software engineer must either compile his or her program for each CPU architecture that users might choose or send the source code to every user for them to compiler on their machines. Neither is a satisfactory solution.

A better solution, which has been applied to a number of languages, is to develop an intermediate step between compilers and interpreters that has the advantages of decent performance and easy portability. For the Java language, the Java program must be translated into what is called byte code, and the byte code can be downloaded and distributed over the Internet. The byte code is a partially compiled program that runs on an abstract or "virtual" machine. The user must use a software program on their machine (the virtual machine software) to run the Java code.

Using this concept, Java programs can be run on any machine that has a "Java virtual machine." An application written in Java is then easily portable to any machine architecture without conflicts, because the application is compiled to run on the virtual machine, not the target machine's CPU architecture. Figure 10.4 illustrates this process.

The universal application and adoption of the Internet and its associated technologies and protocols has accelerated the need for portable applications that can be downloaded from a site on the Internet and run on any machine that has a Java virtual machine.

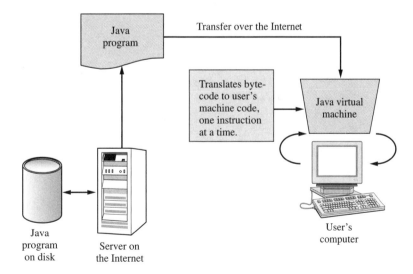

FIGURE 10.4   Java and the Virtual Machine

CHAPTER 10 QUESTIONS

1. Explain the difference between a high-level language and an assembly language.

2. Why is translation necessary?

3. What does a machine-code instruction format do?

4. Using the instruction format explained in Section 10.1, write a machine-code instruction that will add the contents of register 4 with register 5, with the result replacing the contents of register 5.

5. If the opcode for multiply is 000100, write a machine code instruction that will multiply register 2 and register 4, with the result replacing the contents of register 4.

6. What is the difference between an interpreter and a compiler?

7. Why are interpreted languages slower than compiled languages?

8. What are the advantages of the byte code and virtual-machine concept?

9. Search the Web to find and list five compiled languages and the year they were introduced.

10. Search the Web to find and list three interpreted languages and the year they were introduced.

Networking, the Internet, and the World Wide Web

Chapter 11 is an introduction to networking and the Internet, technologies that have transformed how we use computers, expanded their areas of application, and changed our lives. **Prerequisite knowledge needed:** Chapter 8: Machine Architecture.

11.0   INTRODUCTION

The networking of computer systems has profoundly changed the way that we use computers. It has opened up new uses for the machines in assisting humans in obtaining information and new ways for us to interact. The development of the Internet, the Web (and browsers and web pages), email, and distributed computing applications has changed and enriched our lives. This area has an engineering foundation in understanding the electronics and signal processing issues that make fast communication between computers possible. This area also includes management issues: Organizations are now dependent on their computers and the ability to move information from machine to machine for fast communications.

11.1   INTERNETWORKING

Computers have been linked together for the transfer of data since early in the digital age. The ability to move data and information between systems occurred over phone land-lines and dedicated circuits has been common since the 1960s. Moving email between systems is also an old idea, implemented by linking systems together with a dedicated circuit, and allowing systems to pass email messages between themselves.

The Internet is a key concept in the evolution of computing that takes these ideas to the next level, allowing a greater degree of integration of software and data residing on different systems that are geographically distant. The development of the Internet also created powerful applications in the World Wide Web and in the various forms of e-commerce.

The Internet grew out of academic research and research sponsored by the U.S. Department of Defense. The Internet is a system of high-bandwidth links connecting routers, hubs, and gateways, providing extremely fast connectivity between computing machines located anywhere on the planet via Internet access.

The creation of the World Wide Web and hypertext markup language (HTML) resulted in a "killer application" that made the Internet useful for everyone, not just computing professionals and scientists. The hypertext concept was popularized by Apple Computers as a way for computer users to find, organize, and access their data. When extended across the Internet, the Web allows users to find, link to, and access data stored on web pages that can reside anywhere in the world.

DEFINITION OF "INTERNET"

R ESOLUTION: The Federal Networking Council (FNC) agrees that the following
language reflects our definition of the term "Internet": 'Internet' refers to the
global information system that —

  (i)   is logically linked together by a globally unique address space based on the
        Internet Protocol (IP) or its subsequent extensions/follow-ons;
  (ii) is able to support communications using the Transmission Control
        Protocol/Internet Protocol (TCP/IP) suite or its subsequent extensions/follow-
        ons, and/or other IP-compatible protocols; and
  (iii) provides, uses or makes accessible, either publicly or privately, high level services
        layered on the communications and related infrastructure described herein.

—Unanimous resolution, Federal Networking Council, October 24, 1995
www.nitrd.gov/fnc/Internet_res.html

The Internet is a network that links networks of computers or a
metanetwork. It is a dynamically changing interconnection of thousands of
individual networks with millions of computers and users, working through
a standardized set of protocols for data transmission and control of the communications process.

The mechanism that provides the service to route packets between
source and destination is in these two protocols that are the key innovation in
building the Internet: Transmission Control Protocol (TCP) and Internet Protocol (IP), which together are called TCP/IP. The architecture of the Internet
is designed to interconnect networks through these standardized protocols.
The TCP/IP protocol pair is designed to connect any networks together, regardless of the specific hardware and internal protocols running internal to
those networks. By adding the TCP/IP protocols and creating a physical connection with the Internet, any node on any connected network can communicate seamlessly with any other node on the interconnected networks.

TCP/IP is an open standard, allowing any company to produce hardware
and software that is compatible with the Internet and to allow it to grow and
develop on an unprecedented scale.

The architecture of the Internet is a complex weaving of many networks interconnected at multiple levels. The Internet backbone consists of multiple
very-high bandwidth communication links, which handle the long-distance
transfer of information and are operated by large telecommunications companies. Many cross-connections between backbone sections and bandwidth
providers create multiple redundant paths through the Internet. Many branches
and subbranches connect either directly or indirectly to the Internet backbone.

Data moves through the Internet in packets, which can be routed from segment to segment automatically by network routing computers that rely on the Internet's addressing protocol. Each network and each machine on the Internet has a unique address, so that any computer in the world that is connected to the Internet can be identified unambiguously. Starting from the source, each communication packet is routed up in the hierarchy of interconnected networks and is then routed back down through the networks to its destination. Routing within both the source and destination networks is provided by the local network, while Internet service providers and backbone operators provide the routing at the higher levels.

11.2   BASIC NETWORKING CONCEPTS

To be networked computers must be able to transfer information between each other. This requires:

- **Medium:** Computers are networked through a physical medium, whether a network cable, Internet provider, wireless network, and so forth.
- **Protocol:** A protocol is a plan or set of standards for arranging bits so that both source and destination have the same expectations for formatting data. The protocol includes a frame or packet definition. Frames and packets are the names used for the definition of how the bits and bytes will be organized and grouped together to be transmitted as a group (as a frame or packet).
- **Control protocol:** This is the strategy that will be used to allow multiple machines to share the transmission medium in a logical way. The control protocol may be involved in providing fair access, so that all machines have a chance to use the shared media. The control protocol also is involved in determining the quality of service that includes verifying that packets have been received and received correctly.

11.3   ETHERNET

One of the most common networking protocols/standards is ethernet. Ethernet is a relatively old standard, with its origins dating back to World War II—for use in setting up a network or radios that share a common set of frequencies.

With ethernet, there is a common shared media that could be cable, twisted-pair, wireless (radio frequency), or other ways to send signals between machines. The basic control strategy to govern the use of that shared media can be described with an acronym: CSMA/CD. CSMA/CD stands for

- **Carrier Sense:** A machine that needs to send data will first listen to the media to see if it is idle or in use (i.e., listen before talk).
- **Multiple Access:** Multiple devices can share the use of the medium by following these rules for access.
- **Collision Detection:** Even when machines listen to the media for it to be idle before transmitting, there is a possibility that more than one machine can transmit on top of each other, called a *collision*. This occurs when multiple machines are waiting for the media to become idle when an ongoing transmission completes. More than one machine may detect that the medium is idle at the same time and may begin to transmit. Multiple machines transmitting at the same time result in garbled signals so that none of the messages gets through correctly. It is critical that collisions be detected when they occur so that frames containing data can be retransmitted. Collisions are detected by having the transmitting machines monitor the media while transmitting and comparing the signals actually on the media to what it is sending (listen while talk). If the signals don't match, a collision has occurred. When a collision is detected, all transmitting machines will immediately cease transmission and will send a jamming signal to ensure that all machines detected either the collision or the jamming signal. Then, the transmitting machines wait a random amount of time (in order to space out the retransmissions) and then listen for the media to go idle in order to retransmit.

One of the interesting features of the ethernet protocol is that its behavior is nondeterministic; in other words, its performance will vary depending on the quantity of traffic. The more traffic on the network, the greater the chance of accidental collisions. Each collision wastes bandwidth both during the collision and through the jamming signals and subsequent retransmission. Therefore, as an ethernet system approaches heavy use and collisions consume more and more bandwidth, its efficiency and useful bandwidth begins to decline.

There are protocols that do not suffer the performance degradation under heavy load that is characteristic of ethernet, but at the cost of a more complex protocol and logic. Ethernet became widely adopted due to its initial lower cost to manufacture network controllers compared to more complicated protocols that perform more efficiently, when that manufacturing cost differential was a very large competitive advantage. Ethernet won in the marketplace and has since become a universal standard in spite of its performance limitations. Advanced ethernet technologies have pushed the technology to every higher speeds in spite of the original performance-limiting design. The study of advanced networking protocols will include interesting techniques and strategies.

Figure 11.1 illustrates the structure of an ethernet frame. The frame is divided into fields, each with a different meaning. The first field (START) is a preamble that the network cards use to synchronize to the patter of

START	DEST	SOURCE	T	DATA	FRAME

FIGURE 11.1   Ethernet Frame

transmission bit signals. The DEST and SOURCE fields are the address of the destination and source machines. The T field is for the type of frame. The DATA field can be of variable length, holding from 46 to 1500 bytes of data. The final field is a frame-check sequence that is used to check for transmission errors.

The SOURCE and DESTINATION (DEST) fields are each six bytes long (48 bits), allowing 2^{48} (256 trillion) different addresses, which far exceeds the number of humans on the planet. This very large number of different possible addresses seems excessive, considering that the number of network nodes (machines) on a single ethernet network is performance limited, though more recent ethernet variations have much greater capacities and speeds than the original design. The reason for the large number of possible addresses is to allow the assignment of blocks of addresses to different network interface board manufacturers, in order to guarantee that no ethernet board would be sold that duplicates another address on an existing board. This also guarantees that as technology advances, old boards can be thrown away and replaced with new ones without worrying about recovering or "trading-in" the old ethernet addresses for reassignment and reuse.

11.4   INTERNETWORKING PROTOCOLS

As mentioned in Section 11.1, the protocol developed to interconnect networks is TCP/IP, where TCP stands for transmission control protocol and IP stands for internetwork protocol. These protocols were designed to work with existing networking protocols (like ethernet) and not to replace them. TCP/IP encapsulates networking protocols: Basically, the lower level data transmission frame is "chopped up" into pieces called *packets*. Then, each packet receives a "wrapper" that includes the TCP/IP addressing and control information needed to span the Internet from network to network.

Figure 11.2 illustrates how data is encapsulated with control information at each level of protocol. The data is first encapsulated with the TCP control information in a header. That combined control/data packet is then presented to the next protocol layer (IP) as data and receives another header around it. Finally, the packet with both IP and TCP control information is presented to the lowest networking-level protocol (ethernet, for example) and is further encapsulated with another layer of control information. This process of encapsulation can go on for multiple levels—in fact, some applications encapsulate control information along with the data itself.

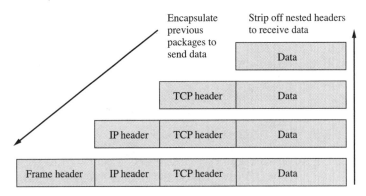

FIGURE 11.2 Encapsulation

At each level of transmission and reception, the protocol headers are either added when transmitting or stripped off when receiving.

11.5   THE WORLD WIDE WEB

The World Wide Web is a way of using the Internet to request and retrieve information and to interact with remote computer systems. The Web could be considered to be an application on the Internet. The Web consists of four concepts:

1. **Markup language:** This is the language that specifies codes that allow the developer to format the appearance of web pages. The web browser must understand and be able to interpret these codes, which are standardized as HTML (hyper-text markup language). For instance, to designate that text is to appear in bold, a web page might contain the following line:

   The word <strong> BOLD</strong> is in bold text.

   The <strong> and </strong> are used to begin and end the section of text that is to be displayed as in bold typeface.
2. **Uniform resource locator (URL):** This is a label for the address and location of a page or resource somewhere on the Internet. This label is translated into an actual IP address by servers on the Internet. An example URL is:

   http://www.nsf.gov/

   which is the URL for the U.S. government's National Science Foundation.

3. **Hypertext or Hyperlinks**: These are embedded links in a web page that can be used to link pages together. The pages can be on different computer systems anywhere on the Internet. Hyperlinks can also be used within a document to allow the users to jump or navigate from place to place within the document quickly. An example of a hyperlink that can be embedded in a web page to link to the Linux operating system organization's home page is:

    <A href=" http://www.linux.org/"> Linux </A>

    Observe that this hyperlink has a URL embedded within it between the double quotes. Note also the use of the markup language < and > to begin and end the HTML commands. The name "Linux" is a label that appears on the web page, and that when clicked on or selected directs the user's browser to go to the URL for the Linux organization.

4. **Client-server model of computing**: This is the idea that an application can be composed of parts that may exist at different machines connected by the Internet that work together. In regards to the Web, there are at least two machines that work together:
    The client machine is the user's PC
    A server with web pages or web applications

    There are a number of other machines that work behind the scenes to make the Internet work and to handle functions like translating the URLs into IP addresses.

CHAPTER 11 QUESTIONS

1. Describe how the Internet works with existing networking protocols.
2. What does the Internet do?
3. Explain in your own words what the World Wide Web is.
4. Consider an alternative approach to the TCP/IP strategy (one that was actually considered): creating a new networking protocol from scratch that can simultaneously be both a networking protocol and an Internetworking protocol. Describe two advantages and disadvantages of this alternative approach.
5. Research the Internet to learn about alternative networking protocols to ethernet. Chose one and describe its functioning using no more than a single page.
6. Explain the concept of encapsulation in regards to networking protocols.
7. Research the World Wide Web and find two URLs of websites that you find interesting.

8. Research the Internet to find two additional HTML codes beyond those presented in this chapter.

9. Research the Internet to find out what XML is. Describe and explain what XML is and how it differs from HTML.

10. Research the Internet to learn what a token-passing networking strategy is.

   a. Describe in your own words what a token-passing network control strategy is.
   b. List one token-passing network control strategy.
   c. List one advantage to a token-passing network control strategy.

PART FOUR

Advanced Computing Concepts

Models of Computation

Chapter 12 is an introduction to the models of computation with two specific examples of computation models that are approachable for new students of computing: Finite State Machine/Finite State Recognizer and Petri Nets. The issue of computability (are there functions that cannot be computed?) is examined briefly. **Prerequisite knowledge needed:** The student must be familiar with a computer system (Chapter 2) and the concepts of basic programming (Chapter 3).

12.0 INTRODUCTION

Computer processing can be modeled in a number of ways using various approaches that range from graphical to algebraic and mathematical. Some models are inherently theoretical, complex, and sophisticated, and require significant study by the programmer in order to become fluent in the technique. Some classical approaches model computer processing with an eye toward understanding if there are limits on what can be computed (there are) and to understand those limitations.

This textbook provides an overview and a sampling of the key concepts in computer science including this theoretical area which is itself composed of many individually complex techniques and approaches, each of which require separate course(s) for complete coverage. Consequently, modeling of computer processing and the question of computability will be touched on only briefly in this chapter. Two specific graphical computing model examples will be covered, which were chosen because they are easy to understand, require no mathematical tools to work, are applicable in problem solving and analysis in general, and are used in computer architecture specifically, in finite state machines and petri nets.

12.1 FINITE STATE MACHINES

Computability is the study of problem types, primarily from a formal and mathematical point of view, and includes formal methods for representing problems. Of interest are the problem types that have no solution; also of interest are the how resources required scale with the problem size.

In addition, computability includes formal models of computing, including finite automaton, push-down automaton, turning machines, regular languages, and finite state machines.

Finite state machines (FSM) will be examined in this chapter as an example of this fascinating area of study. FSMs can be presented casually without an extensive formal mathematical presentation (reserved for later computing classes). FSMs also have application in a number of areas in computing including computer architecture, data communications, and embedded systems. Thus, the student of computing is likely to encounter this conceptual model of computing in other areas of study, where it has use as a tool for defining and solving problems.

An FSM is a model for representing computing as inputs causing the current state to change to a new change. This is a graphical model, where states are represented as circles, and the inputs and the changes to new states represented by arrows which connect the states.

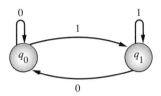

FIGURE 12.1   Finite State Machine

Figure 12.1 illustrates a very simple FSM. It has just two states, which represent two ideas:

1. The most recent input to the machine is a zero.
2. The most recent input to the machine is a one.

The inputs to the machine are clearly either zero or one; no other inputs are possible.

If the machine is in state q_0 and receives a "1" as its input, it will transition to state q_1. If the machine is in state q_1 and receives a "0" as its input, it will transition to state q_0.

If the machine is in state q_0 and receives a "0" as its input, it will stay in the same state q_0. If the machine is in state q_1 and receives a "1" as its input, it will stay in the same state q_1. Therefore, regardless of the sequence of inputs of 0 or 1, the machine will always be in the state that indicates the last input that the machine received.

12.2 FOUR-STATE FSM

A more complex machine can be created that recognizes a sequence of inputs of zero and one. As an example, consider a machine that "looks for" the pattern of inputs "101" (Figure 12.2):

This machine has four states: q_0, q_1, q_2, and q_f. State q_f is the "final" state, that indicates that the looked for sequence of zeros and ones has been "seen" in the input stream.

From state q_0, the only way to get to state q_f is through a sequence 1, 0, 1. A meaning can be assigned to each of the states that notes how much of the intended sequence of zeros and ones has actually been observed at this point:

State q_0: has received zeros so far.
State q_1: has received the first "1" in the sequence.
State q_2: has received a "10" so far.
State q_f: has received the complete sequence of "101."

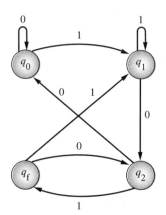

FIGURE 12.2   Four-State Finite State Machine

When inputs are received out of sequence, they cause the machine to fall back to other states. For instance, when in state q_2, the machine is "looking for" a final "1." If it receives a "0" instead, it has now received two zeros in a row "00," which is not a part of the desired sequence. The machine falls back to q_0, and must repeat the process of looking for the first 1 in an uninterrupted sequence of 101. The reader should examine each state and consider each of the two possible inputs, zero or one, to confirm that the machine is transitioning to the next correct state.

FSMs are interesting because they can represent many useful machines. A classic example is a soda machine that collects nickels, dimes, and quarters until it receives the cost of a soda, say $0.60, at which point it "recognizes" that a drink has been paid for and dispenses one to the customer. This machine has more than two coin inputs, it has three: nickels, dimes, and quarters. Multiple combinations of inputs can total to $0.60: six dimes, two quarters and a dime, and so forth, so there are multiple ways to get to the "final" soda-dispensing state. A final complication for this machine is that the customer could put in more money than exactly $0.60—say, three quarters. This machine will need to give change as well as dispense soda as its outputs. The student is encouraged to play with this idea to build a finite state machine for this problem.

FSMs can be used in building computer systems at more than one level. Wherever a sequence of inputs is intended to cause specific outcomes, an FSM may be a useful design tool. FSMs are used to build simple digital logic circuits, where the FSM is a specification for what the hardware is intended to do, and a hardware implementation of the FSM is then constructed. FSMs can be useful in data communications and networking, where bits are being transmitted in a sequence, and parts of the bit stream transmit an address for the destination, the data, and other control information. FSMs can scan the incoming stream of bits for particular control sequences of bits that are used to signal the receiving device.

12.3 PETRI NETS

Another interesting yet simple to understand way to model computing is with petri nets. Petri nets visually show a system that can change states, as FSMs do, but can also show the movement of things through a system. In addition to using circles to represent states and arrows to represent changes to other states, petri nets can represent both control issues and the movement of material through a system.

A simple example will illustrate the power and usefulness of this model. Figure 12.3 illustrates a system that consists of two entities: a producer and a consumer. As an abstract example it is not important to know what specifically is being produced and consumed; it could be data packets or LCD screens on a cell-phone production line or any other manufactured item.

The producer–consumer of Figure 12.3 illustrates transitions between states. *Transitions* are events that have preconditions; that is, there are conditions that must be met before the transition can be made. Constraints can be met by providing the required article or permission, both represented by a "token," which is a small circle.

Figure 12.3 does not show the tokens that move through the system and represent states. As tokens move through the system (and as the producer and consumer change the "state" that they are in), the tokens must cross

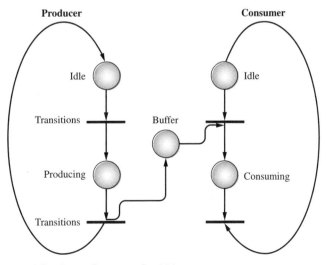

FIGURE 12.3 Producer–Consumer Petri Net

transitions. Each transition will consume and create tokens. Each arrow feeding into a transition requires a token. A transition that has two arrows feeding will require a token to be present at each of the states at the base of the arrows before it can proceed. The consumer has a state that requires a token to be in the consumer's "idle" state (showing that the consumer is idle) and a token must be in the shared buffer between the producer and consumer.

Each transition will create as many tokens as it has arrows leading from it. The producer has a transition that has only one arrow leading into it, but two arrows leading out. When this transition "fires," a single token will create two tokens. Creating a new token out of nothing is OK, because the tokens can mean different things at different times. In this case one token is used to show the state that the producer is in while the other token represents an object that was created and is now ready for consumption.

Figure 12.4 shows the produce–consumer system with both the producer and the consumer in their idle states. Notice that for the producer to transition to the producing state, it need only be in the idle state (represented by a token in the idle state bubble). On the other hand, the consumer cannot transition to the consuming state without a token in the buffer as well (it needs to have something available to consume). In order to cross a transition, tokens must be present in all states at the source of each arrow.

Figure 12.5 shows the producer–consumer after the producer has completed its production process. The producer has placed a token in the buffer, ready for the consumer. The consumer now has tokens in each state preceding its transition.

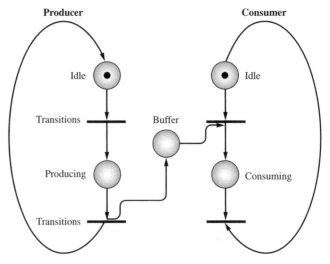

FIGURE 12.4   Initial State

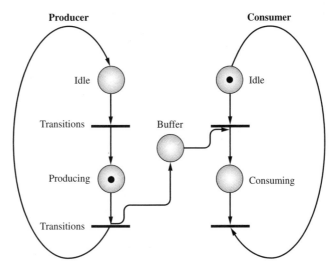

FIGURE 12.5 Production

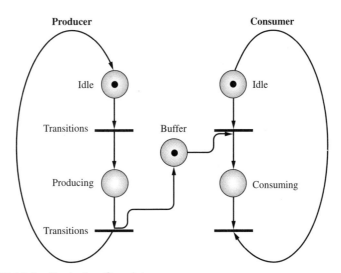

FIGURE 12.6 Production Complete

Figure 12.6 shows that production is now complete, and both the producer and consumer are in their idle states. Note that now the consumer may begin its consumption because there are tokens both in the idle state and in the shared buffer.

Figure 12.7 shows that the consumer is now in the process of consuming, while the producer has simultaneously begun to produce another item. Note that the token that was in the shared buffer has been consumed.

Figure 12.8 shows that the producer and consumer are both now ready to repeat the cycle: The producer can proceed to production again, while the consumer has what it needs to begin consumption of the item in the shared buffer.

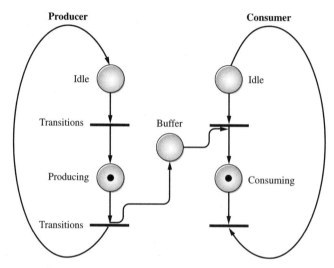

FIGURE 12.7   Consumption and Production

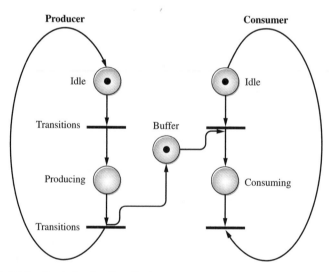

FIGURE 12.8   Ready for Another Cycle

12.4 COMPUTABILITY

This section examines the question of whether all functions that can be described can also be computed. In other words, are there functions that exist that are not computable?

To be computable means that a function can be implemented with a program or algorithm that works and produces the correct result in finite time. A related but different question is whether a function can be computed in an acceptable amount of time. A function that takes 1,000 years of computation to complete would be computable, but would not have a practical or usable program/algorithm implementation.

This section will proceed by first examining this concept: that given that the number of possible functions is infinite, and the number of existing programs at any given time is finite, there must be some (actually infinitely many) functions that do not have programs in existence.

This is a weak argument because the case could be that programs have simply not been written *yet* for any specific function, but *could* be written if needed, thus proving that the specific function in question is computable. If this is indeed the case, it does not prove that all functions are computable, but it does undermine the argument that there *must* be noncomputable functions.

A better way to explore noncomputability is to demonstrate that there exists at least one function that cannot be computed. The noncomputable function that we will consider is related to the "halting problem."

The *halting problem* can be explained in this way: Consider programs that are designed to read other programs. The code for the subject programs is input to these programs, similar to the way that word-processing documents are inputs (and outputs) to the word-processing application program. The class of programs that can read other programs are called *meta-programs*.

The first version of these meta-programs will determine if the subject program will halt or go on forever. Programs that do not halt get "stuck" in infinite loops and are generally considered to be failures and incorrectly written. A pseudocode example of a program that does not halt follows:

```
WHILE 0 = 0
    Statements
WHILE END
```

This program will never terminate because the condition that controls the loop will always be true. A meta-program to determine if a program will halt must check for all possible infinite loops. This example could have any true statement to be evaluated as the loop condition, and there are an infinite number of possible true statements. No program can be written to identify all possible true statements (there are an infinite number of these) for a loop condition, and there are an infinite number of even more complex programs that are also nonhalting. Therefore, a meta-program that will determine if any possible input program will halt cannot be written. Therefore, the halting problem is noncomputable.

Another similar noncomputable program example is a meta-program to determine whether two subject programs are equivalent. Because it is not possible to determine whether a program will halt or not, two programs that cannot be determined to halt cannot be compared for equivalency. Thus a meta-program to determine if two programs are equivalent is noncomputable.

CHAPTER 12 QUESTIONS

1. Build an FSM that recognizes a sequence of binary inputs: "110."
2. Build an FSM that recognizes the sequence of binary inputs "1101." This may require fives states.
3. What would be the result if the buffer state were removed in the producer–consumer petri net model?
4. The petri net producer can also be constrained from production by adding a buffer that represents and available storage location. Draw a revised producer–consumer petri net with this constraint added.
5. Build a petri net model of some simple process that you are familiar with. You might choose to model a single entity or process (the producer-consumer model showed two interacting entities).
6. Explain in your own words what it means to be noncomputable.

Artificial Intelligence

C hapter 13 is an introduction to the diverse and complex field of artificial intelligence. **Prerequisite knowledge needed:** Chapter 12: Models of Computation.

13.0 INTRODUCTION

Artificial intelligence is the field within computing dedicated to the idea of building computers that can think for themselves, independent of human intervention. Substantial progress has been made in this area (which is highly theoretical and highly complex) by following the approach of "capturing" human intelligence and rendering it into a form that the machine can follow.

Whether "artificial intelligence" has been created in this way or whether the machines are simply being made to mimic the way humans think is an open question for philosophical discussion. This is a fascinating area with much challenging and exciting work ahead.

13.1 ARTIFICIAL INTELLIGENCE

Artificial intelligence is the investigation into building computing systems that appear to be intelligent. The study of artificial intelligence predates the modern electronic computer, with early thinkers investigating the possibility of mechanical thinking machines. We don't truly understand what intelligence is, but we hope we know it when we see it. To build artificial intelligence turns out to be a rather clouded goal that we must feel our way toward. Because we do not truly understand the goal of achieving artificial intelligence, a more pragmatic goal has been accepted: Systems that exhibit behavior that mimics human decision making, and systems that behave rationally, can be said to be artificially intelligent.

What is intelligence? We are at the early stages of understanding what makes human intelligence: Does human intelligence arise autonomously from assembling a sufficient number of neurons together in a brain—a sort of, "The whole is greater than the sum of the parts"? If so, then building computers with sufficient processing capability to match the complexity of the human brain may result in generating an artificially intelligent computer.

Perhaps human intelligent awareness is a process—a change of state over time in an extremely complex FSM or petri net. Consciousness generates detectable patterns of electrical waves as neurons fire and communicate in a cyclic pattern within the human brain. Perhaps establishing a similar cyclic pattern of repetitive waves of communication can create a system that becomes intelligent. As we think to ourselves in our language, we are formulating ideas and concepts that evolve over time. Perhaps a sufficiently complex system with multiple levels of feedback and sufficient memory to hold our current "state" will generate intelligent behavior.

Our efforts to create artificial intelligence are hampered in that we have only one example to work from as a basis: human intelligence, which we only barely understand. We long have had mathematical models and systems for dealing with logic and logical problem solving. We can build systems that can process according to rules of logic. Then, by representing facts and relationships using symbols that can be entered into a computer's memory, the computer can manipulate the symbols according to the rules of logic also entered into the machine. Computers have had this type of capability for decades, but it is not considered to be proof of intelligence. The computer does not understand what the symbols mean nor the meaning of any conclusions that it arrives at. The computer in this system is simply manipulating digital data according to a fixed set of rules.

The complexity and our lack of understanding of what intelligence is has long befuddled investigators predicting intelligent machines, typically 10 years in the future. In fact, researchers in the 1950s expected intelligent computers in a decade; in the 1960s they expected it in the 1970s, in the 1970s it was predicted for the 1980s, and so on. In the 1980s, Japan began a national effort to create the fifth generation of computers—artificially intelligent, with the stated goal of jumping ahead of the competition and researchers in other nations. That major effort obtained some worthwhile results and contributed to our understanding of artificial intelligence, but failed to create a new generation of intelligent computers and so failed in its strategic purpose. (Perhaps Japan's leadership in domestic and industrial robotics will achieve their strategic goal in the 2010s.)

The remainder of this chapter is a high-level overview of the various fields of study within artificial intelligence (AI).

13.2 PROBLEM SOLVING AND COMPLEX ALGORITHMS

One early approach to AI centered on finding clever and efficient ways to solve extremely complex problems, particularly those problems that have no clear solution, and problems sufficiently complex as to require an excessive amount of time to solve (perhaps years of processing time). Typically, these problems are manifested as a problem with no mathematical solution, but the number of possible solutions are far too large for even a fast computer to examine them all in a search for the best solution.

A classic example is the traveling salesman problem. Here, a salesman must travel to visit clients in many cities, each separated geographically by a different number of miles. The problem or goal is to find the best order of cities to visit, which minimizes the number of miles traveled. The problem is easy enough to state, but for more than just a few cities, the problem becomes too large to be solvable in reasonable time using the "brute force" method of looking at all possible solutions and ranking them. This is because the number of possible solutions that would have to be examined increases at an exponential rate. With two cities (see Table 13.1), there are

TABLE 13.1 Cities and Routes

Cities	1st	2nd	3rd	4th	# of routes
Two cities (A and B)	A	B			2 routes
	B	A			
Three cities (A, B, and C)	A	B	C		6 routes
	A	C	B		
	B	A	C		
	B	C	A		
	C	A	B		
	C	B	A		
Four cities (A, B, C, and D)	A	B	C	D	24 routes
	A	B	D	C	
	A	C	B	D	
	A	C	D	B	
	A	D	B	C	
	A	D	C	B	
	B	A	C	D	
	B	A	D	C	
	B	C	A	D	
	B	C	D	A	
	B	D	A	C	
	B	D	C	A	
	C	A	B	D	
	C	A	D	B	
	C	B	A	D	
	C	B	D	A	
	C	D	A	B	
	C	D	B	A	
	D	A	B	C	
	D	A	C	B	
	D	B	A	C	
	D	B	C	A	
	D	C	A	B	
	D	C	B	A	

TABLE 13.2   Combinatorial Explosion

Cities	n!
5	120
6	720
7	5040
8	4030
10	3,628,800
20	2,432,902,008,176,640,000

just two alternatives. With three cities there are six, and with four cities there are more.

The relationship between the number of cities to be visited, and the number of possible routes to be examined is n factorial (***n!***), where n is the number of cities to be visited. Informally, n factorial is the product of n terms, each of which is one less than the previous. For example, $3! = 3 \times 2 \times 1 = 6$; $4! = 4 \times 3 \times 2 \times 1 = 24$. For even larger numbers, n factorial grows extremely large (Table 13.2).

Clearly, even a modest number of cities (20) generates too many possible routes to exhaustively check every possible solution via a "brute force" approach to find the best one in a reasonable period of time.

The brute force method of checking every possible solution won't do. The study of clever ways reduce the problem by skipping some of the possible solutions from the need to be checked is part of this approach to AI. Other approaches to these intractable problems are not intended to obtain the exact best solution, but will at least return a good solution in a reasonable amount of time.

13.3   GAME PLAYING

Computer game playing has long been a forum for testing our ability to create computer programs that behave intelligently. Early approaches to game playing involved quantifying the game as a discrete problem that can be represented on a computer and then letting the computer explore possible solutions. Simple games like tic-tac-toe and checkers have been solved.

More complex games like chess are approached with a combination of brute force searching for solutions combined with ways to eliminate sections of possible solutions from needing to be checked, along with observation of human chess players and recognizing patterns in the arrangements of the pieces on the board that lead to likely avenues to explore and negative outcomes not worth exploring.

Complex games like chess experience the same kinds of combinatorial explosion in possible solutions (i.e., factorial and other) as the traveling salesman problem. The best computer players are now competitive with the very best human player and will soon be superior.

As an example, consider a game that might have 10 game pieces for each opponent. Each piece can move to any of 10 different locations on the game board. For the first player, there are 10×10 or 100 possible moves. For each of those possible moves, the opponent (who has 10 pieces, each of which can move to 10 different locations) may make 100 possible moves as well. That leads to 100×100 possible situations after each player takes a single turn. A third turn will generate 100^3 possible outcome situations. Granted, in a real game, some moves may eliminate game pieces, some moves may be illegal, and so forth, which does cut down on the number of moves to explore.

There are war game enthusiasts who refight historical military battles, involving as many as 100 or more game pieces (representing military units) for each side. Some game pieces may be able to move to any of 100 or more locations. Each military unit also has multiple actions it can take in addition to simply moving (attacking, rearming, reorganizing, etc.). Clearly, then, there are games that are even more complex than chess in terms of the number of possible solutions to explore. Humans can deal with these types of games in a variety of ways without the brute-force power of computers, many of which are being mimicked in computer game playing. Some of these methods involve specialized knowledge about the situation (military strategy and tactics); others involve ways to reason about uncertainty, and still others involve finding good solutions without guaranteeing finding the best solution.

13.4   MACHINE LEARNING

If a computer program can reliably defeat the best human opponents in a complex game like chess, has it achieved artificial intelligence? Early researchers thought that accomplishment might signal the creation of artificial intelligence. Modern researchers, however, do not believe this is artificial intelligence, but merely human intelligence in creating the rules and programming that allows the computer to play well. Human intelligence has been "captured" and installed in a computer program so that it plays the game the way the human specifies it should. Perhaps if the computer could learn to play chess on its own at the grand master level through machine learning, then one might maintain that the ability to self-learn how to play a complex game might signal intelligence. Machine learning is the investigation into how a computer and program can learn.

How do humans learn? Educational experts will argue that there are a variety of styles of learning that people use with each person generally favoring one method over another.

A general approach to machine learning requires:

- an initial set of rules and knowledge about the environment in which the machine will operate.
- the ability to observe the environment and identify and detect objects in that environment.
- the ability to manipulate that environment.
- the ability to record new facts through exploration of the environment and changes that occur.
- the ability to generate and add new rules or learning to its existing set of knowledge about the environment and how to manipulate it.

13.5 EXPERT SYSTEMS AND NEURAL NETWORKS

Expert systems are one of the first commercialized applications of AI. The idea is to capture the expert knowledge of a human expert as a set of rules stored in a database or knowledge base. That stored expert knowledge then is used by the expert systems engine to answer questions, diagnose problems, and guide others in decision making. Expert systems have been applied in many areas, from diagnosis of disease to capturing the expertise of a head chef to guiding technicians through the repair of a computer or other equipment.

An expert system consists of an expert systems engine and a knowledge base. The engine can be developed using conventional programming languages or a commercial system can be purchased. The knowledge of the expert is then captured and recorded in the knowledge base as a set of rules with some data. The process of capturing the knowledge of an expert as rules requires expertise in working with the expert systems engine, depending on the sophistication of the engine. A simple system will require the formulation and entering of the rules and then organizing the rules into a structure that determines which rule is active under specific circumstances. This can be a bit tricky and may require the use of nonstandard programming control structures to process and search through the rules.

Neural networks attempt to build logical structures that function the way neurons in the brain function, with many connections between neurons. Neural networks can be implemented entirely in software, as a simulation of a neural network, thus allowing the network to be changed and rewired as needed. Alternatively, a neural network can be implemented with hardware and processing tailored for this function.

The simple function of neurons is to take in electrical signals as inputs and then send them out as outputs. Neurons have a threshold level of input required before firing the output. The programming or training of a neural network consists of the pattern of connections between the neurons coupled with the training of the threshold level of the neurons. Neural networks require a training period and training process where responses that are correct are reinforced, and incorrect responses are attenuated.

Neural networks have been applied in a number of domains. Because the neural network is analogous to the neural networks in our brains ("wet-ware," as opposed to hardware), one might surmise that neural networks offer the best opportunity to achieve AI. That remains to be seen; the largest impediment to progress is simply the cost and difficulty of building systems with a sufficiently large number of neurons or simulated neurons. The human brain has trillions of neurons, and as computers continue to grow in size and power, applications of neural networks are likely to expand.

Neural networks are excellent at recognizing patterns (as is the human brain) and so are useful in computer vision, voice recognition, and the like.

13.6   FUZZY LOGIC

Fuzzy logic is reasoning with probabilities. Humans can deal with uncertainty quite well in our decision making, while logic and rule-based systems often stumble with things and relationships are known only with some probability.

The human ability to use fuzzy logic reasoning is one of the ways that humans use to deal with the complexity of problems where a combinatorial explosion excludes direct analysis for a solution. For instance, in the game of chess, humans experts become adept at understanding the patterns of relationships of pieces on the board. Humans do not explore every possible move many turns in the future, but instead guide the pattern of the pieces on the board toward a pattern that is favorable to their side. In making these kinds of decisions, humans use reasoning about the probable moves of their opponent because future moves are unknown. In fact, expert human chess players have used this pattern recognition ability to defeat the best machine chess players, by learning the patterns of responses that the computer will make in various situations and then taking advantage of that knowledge to control the course of the game.

Basically, every fact stored in a computer using fuzzy logic is associated with a probability of it being true (which could be 100%), but the rules and relationships that the computer uses to reason about the environment also accommodates probabilities of the inputs or premises of a rule, and then generates a probability of the conclusion or outcome of a rule being true.

CHAPTER 13 QUESTIONS

1. Consider the classic game tic-tac-toe. Explain the type of artificial intelligence you might utilize to build a computer program to play this game.

2. What type of AI technology would you use to capture expert knowledge on diagnosing and repairing a home computer?

3. Consider a game in which each player has five pieces that can move each turn. Each piece can move to five different locations. Only one piece can move in a turn.

   a. How many possible moves are there for the first player?

   b. The second player has the same number of moves, in response to each of the possible moves. How many possible situations are there after each player has moved?

   c. If all five of a player's pieces can move in each turn, how many possible situations are there after each player has had one turn?

4. Research the Internet to find a real-world application of AI. Describe that application in a short paragraph.

5. Consider a game where each play can make four different moves in each turn.

   a. How many possible situations are there after one move, two moves, three moves, and four moves?

   b. Can you describe the number of possible situations after n moves with a simple mathematical expression?

Parallel Computation

Chapter 14 covers an introduction to the digital computer as a machine constructed from transistors and logic gates. **Prerequisite knowledge needed:** Chapters 9 and 10.

14.0   INTRODUCTION

Regardless how much faster each generation of computer-chip design increases computing power, there is always a need for more. We seem to have an insatiable need to do more computing in less time. Increasing computing power enables the solution in a timely fashion of problems that would previously be impracticable to solve. Increasing computing power makes it possible to enhance programs with additional features and capabilities that enhance the human–computer interface, such as voice recognition interfaces, 3D graphics, virtual-reality interfaces, and intelligent interfaces.

Each generation of computer-chip design improves performance by miniaturizing the transistors on the chip. Small transistors mean that more can be packed in the same space; in addition, smaller transistors require less energy to operate. Transistors that need less energy to run (often revealed in the voltages necessary to run the devices—5V, 3.3V, 2.2V, 1.1V, 0.7V) generate less heat as wasted energy, allowing a denser packing of transistors without temperatures reaching the failure point. Smaller transistors that operate on less power switch faster and with shorter connections between transistors, allowing chips to operate at higher clock speeds.

Regardless of how physicists and engineers improve our computing devices with each generation (early chips ran at 4,000 cycles per second and less; current chips run at billions of cycles per second), there is a need for more computing power. An alternative approach to achieving higher power is through parallel processing, where multiple processors are combined to complete a workload in less time.

14.1   SIMPLE PARALLEL EXECUTION

Parallel computing systems also offer the possibility of a higher degree of fault tolerance. If a single processor in a system of multiple redundant processors fails, the entire system can continue to function but at reduced power. Redundancy can be applied to many aspect of a computing system, allowing systems with multiple processors, buses, disk drives, memories, caches, network interfaces, and so forth.

Figure 14.1 illustrates the basic concept underlying parallel computing. In this example, there are four processors available for concurrent execution of this process. The process also happens to be dividable into 10 discrete pieces, at most four of which can be executed in different processors concurrently. The process has some set-up work at the beginning that can only be executed on a single processor. Similarly, there is some work at the conclusion of the process when results are collated and consolidated, which must be executed on a single processor.

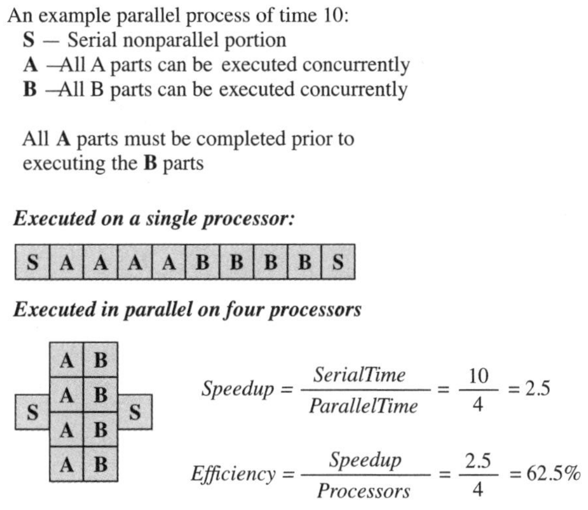

An example parallel process of time 10:
   S — Serial nonparallel portion
   A —All A parts can be executed concurrently
   B —All B parts can be executed concurrently

All **A** parts must be completed prior to
executing the **B** parts

Executed on a single processor:

S	A	A	A	A	B	B	B	B	S

Executed in parallel on four processors

$$Speedup = \frac{SerialTime}{ParallelTime} = \frac{10}{4} = 2.5$$

$$Efficiency = \frac{Speedup}{Processors} = \frac{2.5}{4} = 62.5\%$$

FIGURE 14.1   Execution in Parallel

In Figure 14.1, it is apparent that the process is composed of 10 blocks of processing, each taking the same time for simplicity. When executed on a single processor in serial, it takes 10-time units to complete the work. When taking advantage of the four processors available, to run the same process on the parallel-processing multiprocessor machine the work is completed in only 4-time units.

It is useful to measure the performance improvement of a parallel machine. One measure used is called *speedup*, which is the ratio of the serial time divided by the parallel time. Another performance measure is efficiency, which gives an idea of how much of the available computing power is applied to the problem as opposed to sitting idle. *Efficiency* is the ratio of the speedup obtained on a particular system, over the number of processors or processing elements on the system.

These concepts of parallel processing were first observed by Gene Amdahl, and when formulated a different way are known as *Amdahl's law*. Amdahl's formulation focuses on the fraction or percentage of the workload that can be done in parallel and the percentage that must be completed in serial. These two fractions add up to 100%. The parallel percentage is executed on the parallel processors and will take proportionately less time to complete. The ratio of the serial workload divided by the parallel workload (composed of the parallel and serial fractions) defines speedup.

14.2 AMDAHL'S LAW

In the following formulation, the parallel fraction of the work is represented as alpha, and the serial percentage is then 1-alpha.

$$Speedup = \frac{Serial\ Time}{Parallel\ Time} = \frac{1}{(1-a) + \dfrac{a}{n}}$$

where

$\alpha =$ the fraction of work that can be done in parallel

$1-a =$ the fraction of work that must be done in serial

$n =$ the number of processors

Amdahl's law is not the final word on parallel-processing speedup; it is a simple model that incorporates a number of implied assumptions. These assumptions mean that it is a correct and complete model only for that simplistic model. The following assumptions are implied but not specifically acknowledged in the model; each has historically represented opportunities for investigators to expand our knowledge of parallel processing beyond this baseline model:

- The workload consists of a single process to be executed. *The extension is to consider running multiple programs (processes) simultaneously, where each process may use a different subset of the available processes.*
- The process runs at just one constant degree of parallelism (always uses exactly n parallel processors for the portion of the program that can run in parallel). *The extension is to recognize that many processes will be able to use a varying number of processors, sometimes leaving processors idle and sometimes needing more processors than are available.*
- The process and the work to be completed is constant and will not be scaled up or increased in size in order to take advantage of a larger number of available processors. *The extension recognizes that with a bigger machine (more processors), a* larger workload *may be attempted.*
- Parallelism exists at a single level (Amdahl's model is at the processor level). *Recent work has identified parallelism at five distinct levels, and that the incorporation of multiple simultaneous levels of parallelism yields greater speedups.*

14.3 LIMITATIONS OF PARALLEL PROCESSING

Consider the denominator of Amdahl's law:

$$Speedup = \frac{1}{\left(1-\alpha\right)+\dfrac{\alpha}{n}}$$

The denominator has two parts summed together, only one of which changes as the number of processors (n) changes. Consider the break-point where the two halves of the denominator are equal:

$$\left(1-\alpha\right)=\frac{\alpha}{n}$$

At this point, increasing the number of processors assigned to the task can drive the right half of the equation (α/n) close to zero, thus halving the denominator. Thus, beyond this break-point, the speedup can be at most nearly doubled, even if there is an infinite number of processors available (and assuming the task can utilize an infinite number of processors—a very unlikely condition), and the time required to complete the task can at best be halved.

Beyond this break point, throwing additional processors at a task will produce only limited speedup and time savings. Beyond this break-point the speedup is limited more by α, the fraction of work that can be done in parallel than it is by the number of processors available.

Examples

For $\alpha = 90\%$, the break-point is at

$$\left(1-\alpha\right)=\frac{\alpha}{n} \rightarrow \left(1-0.90\right)=\frac{0.90}{n}$$

Solving for n yields n at 9.

Inserting these values for α and n yields a speedup at the balance point of 5.

Scaling the number of processors toward to drive the α/n toward zero can decrease the denominator approaching 0.10, yielding a speedup approaching 10.

For $\alpha = 99\%$, the break-point is at

$$\left(1-\alpha\right)=\frac{\alpha}{n}\rightarrow\left(1-0.99\right)=\frac{0.99}{n}$$

Solving for n yields n at 99.

For $\alpha = 99.9\%$, the break-point is at

$$\left(1-\alpha\right)=\frac{\alpha}{n}\rightarrow\left(1-0.999\right)=\frac{0.999}{n}$$

Solving for n yields n at 999.

So when in the state where

$$\left(1-\alpha\right)<\frac{\alpha}{n}$$

it may be reasonable to increase the number of processors assigned to the task in order to increase speedup and reduce the time required to complete the task. When

$$\left(1-\alpha\right)>\frac{\alpha}{n}$$

it is not likely to be efficient to allocate additional computing power to the task to return marginal increases in speedup and reductions in time to completion.

This inherent limitation in realizable speedup was observed early on and was considered a discouraging situation, limiting the value in exploring parallel processing. By examining problems and algorithms with very large parallel fractions, it was realized that there are situations where the break-point as defined by $(1 - \alpha)$ is very small, thus allowing the efficient use of a very large number of processors. Many scientific and engineering problems and simulations model systems where the degree of accuracy of the simulation and reliability of the problem solution is increased with very large data sets or very large numbers of points to be simulated. Therefore, there are a large number of problems needing a large number of processors, but by far the most common application of computing for general purposes does not require and may not easily utilize the power of parallel processing. Consequently, most computers and PCs are sold with a single processor or at best a small number of processors or processor-cores. There also are cases where there are a larger number of processors available than can be efficiently utilized, some of which will sit idle as a result. In that case, it makes sense to use the computing resources that would otherwise sit idle, even if doing so is not theoretically efficient.

When the number of available processors is beyond the number utilized efficiently at the break-point, researchers even consider expanding the work to be completed (scaling the work) in order make efficient use of the available processors. Of course this only makes sense when there is real value to be returned by scaling the work to utilize a larger number of processors.

Figure 14.2 illustrates the problem with diminishing returns from parallel processing. The figure charts the efficiency (the parallel speedup divided by the number of processors used) that results with four applications that have different parallel fractions of work. As increasing numbers of processors are allocated to the task, the overall efficiency declines dramatically. Parallel fractions from 80 percent to 99 percent are illustrated. Applications with parallel fractions below 80 percent will result in even worse efficiency, while those with parallel fractions above 99 percent will perform better. There are scientific and engineering number-crunching applications with very high parallel fractions above 99 percent, for which parallel processing is very effective.

The most common approach to realizing greater speedups from parallel processing is by accommodating multiple levels of parallelism on machines that integrate multiple levels of parallel hardware. A fraction of the hardware

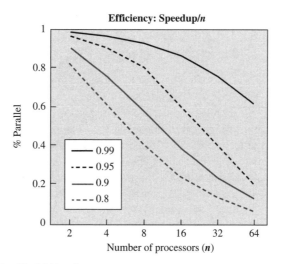

FIGURE 14.2 Diminishing Returns

TABLE 14.1   Levels of Parallelism

Hardware Element	Software Parallelism
Pipeline stages	Intra-instruction
Superscalar: multiple pipelines	Inter-instruction
Multicore: multiple processor "cores" in a chip	Thread/process
Multiple processor on a board or "blade"	Thread/process
Multiple processors/boards/blades in a cluster	Thread/process
Multiple clusters in a system	Thread/process
Multiple "tiers," distributed and grid computing	Process/application

resources is committed to each level instead of all hardware being dedicated at a single level. Thus the parallel speedup realized at each level is toward the more efficient end of the speedup curve and therefore suffers less from the diminishing returns as the number of processing elements increase that is typical of parallel processing.

Note that in Table 14.1 multiple levels of hardware that implement different levels of parallelism at the thread/process level are common, illustrating that "nested" levels or parallelism are possible (i.e., parallel processes may contain parallel threads that each contain grains or blocks of code that can be executed in parallel).

14.4   RELATED AREAS OF EXPLORATION AND GRID COMPUTING

The study of parallel processing also focuses on the architecture of different types of parallel machines. Designs often consist of hundreds or thousands of off-the-shelf processors integrated into a single system. The buses and interconnects that allow the processors to work together are a critical component of a parallel machine because limitations in communication capability severely limit the speedup that can be realized.

Programming languages and operating systems for parallel machines are another related area of study and research. High-level languages that are designed specifically for parallel processing or extensions to existing languages to support parallel processing are needed to support parallel processing, as well as operating systems that are extended or enhanced to coordinate the functioning of many processors.

Parallel programming utilizes programming constructs that are not present in normal (nonparallel) programming. Languages specific to parallel processing have been created, but the most fruitful approach has been to add parallel extensions to an existing programming language. Similarities exist between parallel-programming language features and features required for multithreaded programming. The following example constructs illustrate some of the important programming concepts needed for parallel programming:

> PAR: defines a block of code as executable in parallel and often includes the number of parallel code pieces or threads to create.
> PUBLIC/PRIVATE: used to specify what variables can be shared between parallel sections and what variables are unique to each thread.
> DISTRIBUTE: a mechanism to distribute data sequentially to parallel code pieces, generally by distributing elements or rows/columns of an array.
> SYNCHRONIZE: used to join the parallel threads of execution by forcing waits until all parallel threads or code blocks complete to this point.
> CRITICAL: defines a block of code to be a "critical section" that allows execution by only one thread/processor at a time.

Clustered computing architectures build high-performance multiprocessor machines by grouping processors together in clusters and then combining the clusters together. Clustering processors together works efficiently for a wide range of applications because each cluster contains localized cache or memory storage with a local communication pathway. This architecture compartmentalizes communication traffic and sharing of data within clusters, which allows multiple clusters to be grouped together while avoiding forcing the communication interconnections to become a bottleneck to performance.

Figure 14.3 shows a conceptual diagram of a clustered multiprocessor computer architecture. Four clusters of processors are shown, each with an internal bus and an internal cache memory for high-speed communication and processing within the clusters. The clusters then are interconnected with a second interconnect that not only allows the clusters to communicate

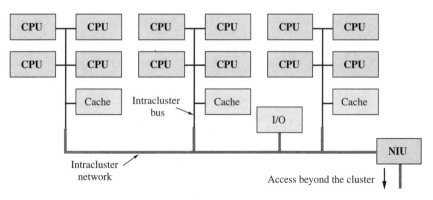

FIGURE 14.3 Clustered Computer Architecture

with other clusters, but also provides access to memory and input and output (I/O) devices. Other cluster configurations are possible with different variations of processors, buses, cache, memory, and disk storage within the cluster (intracluster), and different interconnection topologies to connect the clusters together (Figure 14.3 shows a single bus intercluster interconnect).

One commercially available clustered architecture is a *blade cluster*. Each blade contains two or more processors, for which each processor chip has its own cache, and there is both cache and memory on each blade. The blades are then interconnected with a high-speed network. The physical construction is that each blade is a separate board (like a motherboard) with the processors and components mounted. Multiple blades can be assembled in a chassis backplane, where each blade connects to the backplane for power, intracluster networking, and access outside the cluster to the Internet and other resources.

Figure 14.4 shows a blade-cluster architecture with three blades. Each blade contains two processors, cache, memory, disk storage, and two network interface units. One network interface unit connects to the intercluster network that integrates the clusters into one high-performance machine. One or more blades can be connected to the outside world for communication; generally, one blade is designated as the "master" or controller blade through with the clustered machine communicates with the rest of the world.

Note that the diagram shows two levels of clustering: (1) the cluster of two processors that make up a blade, and (2) the clustering that integrates the blades into a larger machine.

It is also interesting to consider the levels of parallel processing that may exist in a clustered multiprocessor: Each CPU may contain multiple pipelines. A pipeline performs a low level of parallel processing to speed up the processing of instructions (level 1), and each modern processor contains multiple pipelines (level 2). Modern CPU chips are being constructed

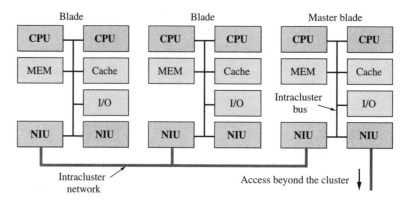

FIGURE 14.4 A Blade-Cluster Architecture

with multiple "cores"; that is, multiple separate processors are integrated together in a single chip and share some components (level 3). The blade cluster illustrated in Figure 14.4 combines two processor chips together on a single blade (level 4), and then combines multiple blades together form the clustered computer (level 5). Multiple-clustered multiprocessors also can be integrated to create an even larger parallel-processing machine with another level of interconnection (level 6). One such implementation design concept is called *grid computing*.

Grid computing is a modern form of distributed computing that coordinates the activities of many parallel processors distributed geographically over a wide area. It is called grid computing because the idea is to create a computing grid similar to the electrical power grid; one simply plugs in and taps the power needed. In grid computing, one accesses the grid with an application and the grid uses available computing power to work the application.

Grid computing involves coordinating and sharing computing resources (often clusters of processors as well as supercomputers), applications, data, and storage. Grid computing is an evolving area of research. Researchers are developing the software technology that seamlessly integrates many machines together to create the grid.

Many researchers and scientific and technology organizations will have occasional need for high levels of computing power, but the cost of assembling an extremely large supercomputer at the needed level of power may be prohibitive. Grid computing offers a solution, where through sharing resources by contributing to the grid organizations then can lay claim to occasionally use the larger resources of the shared grid. Thus, the company avoids the high cost of supercomputing levels of computing power needed only for occasional use and specialized problems.

Note that Figure 14.5 illustrates two critical principles of building high-performance computing systems:

1. *Replication at many levels:* Multiple CPUs on a blade, multiple blades in a cluster, and multiple clusters in a grid.
2. *Interconnection hierarchy:* Multiple interconnects are needed to allow communication between the different levels in an architecture. At each level in hierarchical computer architecture, most of the traffic at that level of device or grouping is local and stays within that device or grouping. Only a small fraction of the communication reaches outside that level.

On a grid system, only a small fraction of the overall communication occurs on the grid interconnect itself (which is most likely the Internet). This allows for the interconnect hierarchy to have different bandwidth capabilities and response times (latency) at each level in order to match the bandwidth required. The overall workload must be balanced across the

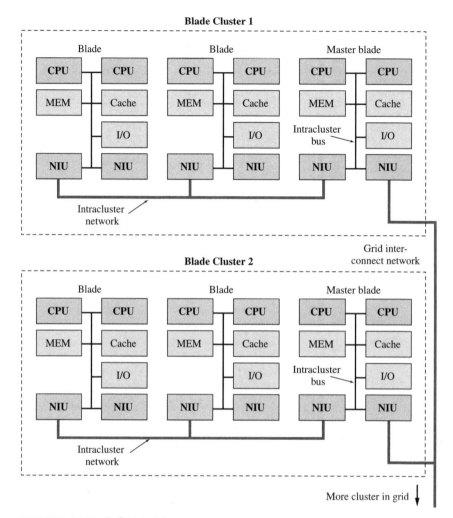

FIGURE 14.5   A Grid Architecture

processors, but just as importantly, the bandwidth requirements must also be balanced across the interconnect hierarchy. Any one interconnect could become a bottleneck that limits overall performance.

Amdahl's simple model of parallel-processing speedup can be extended to allow for the performance effect of the interconnection network latency and contention. Each system will have an average latency for its interconnect while running the parallel workload. The average latency will change depending on how much of the processing requires communication and on the fraction of the communication that occurs at each level of the interconnect. This average depends not only on the system architecture, but also on the characteristics of the workload.

The average latency can be measured in terms of the time to do an instruction; an average latency of one means that each instruction requires an extra delay equal to the processing time of an extra instruction just for the communication. An unlikely average interconnect latency of zero means that the interconnection network performs perfectly or that there is no communication involved. The communication delays force the processor to sit idle while waiting for communication.

$$Speedup = \frac{1}{(1-\alpha) + \alpha L + \dfrac{\alpha}{n}}$$

$\alpha = $ Fraction of work that can be executed in parallel

$n = $ Number of processors or processing elements

$L = $ Average latency over the entire network

Some example speedup values are shown in Table 14.2 for two architectures (with 10 processors and with 1,000 processors).

From the table it is clear that the interconnection network and communication delays can dominate the performance of a parallel system like a grid. This implies that for the best performance, the allocation of the workload across the grid nodes must be done with knowledge of how the application will communicate with other processors in other nodes, so performance bottlenecks that will smother the parallel speedup can be avoided.

TABLE 14.2   Effect of Interconnect Performance on Parallel Speedup

α	n	L	Speedup	
90%	10	0	1/0.19	5.263
90%	10	0.01	1/0.199	5.025
90%	10	0.5	1/0.64	1.563
99%	1000	0	1/0.01099	90.992
99%	1000	0.01	1/0.02089	47.870
99%	1000	0.5	1/0.50599	1.976

CHAPTER 14 QUESTIONS

1. How is parallel processing speedup achieved in general?

2. List and explain what can limit the amount of speedup that can be achieved.

3. **a.** Calculate the speedup using Amdahl's model for a system with 10 processors and a parallel percent of 90.

     b. Calculate the speedup using Amdahl's model, for a system with 100 processors and a parallel percent of 90.

     c. Calculate the efficiency for both 3(a) and 3(b).

4. Describe the architecture of a grid-computing system.

5. Calculate the theoretical performance for a grid system with 256 processors running an application with a parallel fraction of 99.9 percent and a system interconnect average latency of 0.03.

6. Research on the Web one commercial computer system available for sale that contains multiple processing elements (multiple processors or multiple processing cores). Describe the product in a paragraph of your own words.

7. Research on the Web a software product for integrating multiple processors into a single cluster. Describe that software product in a paragraph of your own words.

8. Research on the Web a research grid computing system. Describe that system and its purpose in a paragraph of your own words.

Computing Security

Chapter 15 is an introduction to the issues involving computing security. The technical aspects of security are considered, as well as an overview of security management and policy. **Prerequisite knowledge needed:** Chapter 11: Networking and the Internet.

15.0   INTRODUCTION

Computing security is an important field within computing. It is as old as computing itself, but has received much more attention in the last decade as a result of the proliferation of personal computers connected to the Internet. This has greatly enhanced the usefulness of personal computers but has also greatly expanded access opportunities, so much work has been done to secure systems while much more effort is underway to protect systems in the future.

A theoretical direction in this field is mathematical and focuses on cryptography and the protection and security of valuable data. A more applied direction is toward managing the security process in an organization: building security plans, testing systems for vulnerabilities, and detecting and mitigating threats.

15.1   COMPUTING SECURITY

Though computing security is a relatively new field for intensive study and research, computing systems have allowed for controlled access to data and information since the dawn of computing. This has been accomplished through controlling physical access to systems and through login identifications and passwords. With the rise of the Internet and high-speed communications from anywhere on the globe, computing security risks and attacks have grown dramatically. Rather than computing security being essentially an internal risk (internal to the organization), security issues are now heavily focused on risks and vulnerabilities arising through connectivity to the Internet.

Computing security professionals must identify risks and perform risk assessment and risk analysis. Risks to computing systems arise from a number of sources:

- Natural disasters: fire, flood, storms, earthquakes
- Employee vandalism and corporate espionage
- Hackers/virus/worms, generally through the Internet and revolving around the malicious destruction of data by means of
  Backdoors
  Account/password cracking/spoofing
  Port break-ins
  Software failures/exceptions that allow a redirection that provides access or privileges
  Rarely, physical tapping into a secure network

Figure 15.1 illustrates the many pathways for security access violations. Local users have secured access from inside the organization though networked access or through physical connections directly to the computer

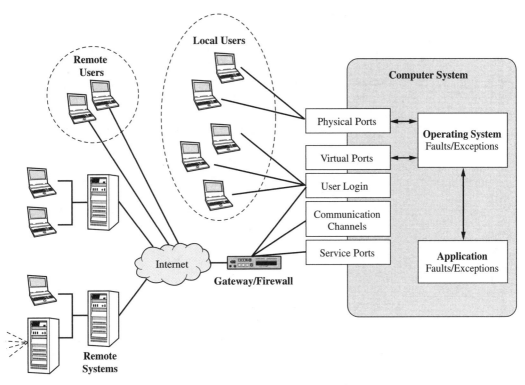

FIGURE 15.1   Security Access

system. Remote users on the Internet can access the system through a set of gateway/firewall devices designed to control and filter access into the system. Other external computer systems may need to access the system through the Internet gateway and firewall for exchanging data and information. External systems may also have users on those systems and are themselves connected to other systems and users. The Internet allows users from anywhere in the world to access the system, and persons with malicious intent will often access the system through multiple levels of indirect access through other systems for concealment.

15.2   SECURITY TECHNOLOGIES

Security technologies include:

    Login/Password: Users must be granted a login ID and secure password in order to obtain access into the systems. Passwords should be relatively complex to prevent break-ins by means of trying all combinations. Large numbers of possible combinations with passwords requiring a combination of letters, numbers, and special symbols greatly increase the number of possible combinations that would need to be tried to guess a password, leading to the early detection of break-in attempts. Passwords should be double-blind so that persons with system-level access authorization can not see other users' passwords.

Controlled physical access: This includes controlling access directly to the computer system, and controlling physical access to local networks with direct physical connections to the computer system, as well as through controlling access to buildings and offices with PCs that have access to the computer system without going through the Internet (and thus the gateway/firewalls).

Gateways/firewalls: There are a variety of computing devices that are used to control access though the Internet to a computing system. These devices can be screen/filter access to allow specific IP address and to prevent or allow specific domains. Specific service-type requests can be prevented/allowed/screened to prevent/allow activities such as remote file transfer and distributed database access.

Antivirus software: Installed on all machines to detect and protect against viruses and worms.

Encryption: A set of technologies to encrypt data for transmission and to control access through a set of public and/or private keys that ensure that only the intended receiver can decrypt encrypted transmissions.

Backups: Duplicating data on backup devices or backup media is a fundamental technique for protecting data. Backup copies of data can be used to ensure that a loss or corruption of data damages only the most recent changes to the data. Systems can be restored to the point of the last backup. Backups are generally done at least daily, with a copy of the recent backups maintained to guard against the case where a data corruption goes undetected over multiple days. To guard against physical disaster and acts of nature, a backup copy is stored offsite in a secure and protected location.

15.3 SECURITY POLICY AND MANAGEMENT

Examination of Figure 15.1 reveals a number of points of possible failure clustered at the interface/boundary of each component:

Applications: Traditionally, applications have been designed for capabilities, performance, and maintainability, but not for security. The design of secure applications involves examining each object/ module for failure conditions and handling each condition within the code itself rather than causing a fault to the operating system. The design of secure applications is a relatively new concept and is currently an evolving area of computer science, focusing on software-design methodologies that facilitate the creation of software that internally handles all exceptions in a controlled and predictable fashion.

Operating system: Depending on the circumstances, some application and system faults can be exploited by users intending to break in the system, so that the process that experiences the fault ends up with system-level privileges, allowing the trespasser the power to destroy or steal. This problem is combatted by ensuring that applications and system processes have mechanisms for handling faults and failures gracefully, so the process ends in a controlled state. This is difficult to do, especially for large applications, because it involves a detailed analysis of all possible mechanisms for the software to fail either fully or partially, which is a time-intensive process.

Ports/device connections: These include the physical and virtual ports that allow communication with the computing system. Physical access ports can be secured through physical security, while virtual ports to the system—operating-system and services—are both more numerous and more dangerous. Software tools are available to control access to each port and service at a fine level, but require system administrator attention. Interestingly, many applications create internal system accounts and server access points during the installation that must also be examined and controlled.

Gateway/firewall access: These devices are designed to filter and protect systems from attack through the Internet; they are not generally vulnerable points themselves, but are instead key tools in building secure systems.

Security policy and management is a management of information systems task that falls on all systems and network administrators. The process starts with an identification of all vulnerabilities and access points and the development of a plan and standards for monitoring and protecting all systems features. A strong plan includes an in-depth defense that secures all access vulnerabilities against attack and failure, rather than relying on a single tool (like a firewall) alone. The plan should include monitoring processes and procedures to detect failures and attacks, which includes examining log files for unusual and unexplained activities. Much of the detection process can be automated, but human oversight is required to handle new attacks and techniques not previously seen. Response plans to each attack/failure/disaster must be developed and included in the overall planning and management of the computing systems.

CHAPTER 15 QUESTIONS

1. List three points where a computer system might be vulnerable (refer to Figure 15.1 for ideas).

2. For each point listed in Question 1, describe at least one technique or process to mitigate the vulnerability you identified.

3. Describe the elements of an information security and assurance plan.

4. Research antivirus software on the Web. List two companies that design antivirus software.

5. A related topic is the concept of computer forensics. Research this topic on the Web and write a short paragraph explaining the idea behind computer forensics.

Applying Computing

This chapter touches on just a few areas where computing technology can be applied to improve the quality of our lives. **Prerequisite knowledge needed:** Chapter 2.

16.0   INTRODUCTION

Information systems is the application of computing technologies along with people and procedures to organizations and problems in specific areas and industries. The foundation is to process more work faster, cheaper, and more reliably through the application of computing technologies in a planned and managed process. Computing technologies have been applied in many different domains, some of which are now recognized as separate areas of specialization and research, job classification, and academic disciplines.

16.1   BUSINESS INFORMATION SYSTEMS AND MANAGEMENT OF INFORMATION SYSTEMS

Business information systems is the general name for the application of people, technologies, and procedures to business problems. *Management of information systems* (MIS) is the idea of managing the resources in a business information system—an area that developed in the gap between computer science and business administration. To effectively apply computing in business, the computer scientist must understand the needs and goals of the business organization, while business managers and experts need to understand the strengths and weaknesses of computing systems and the abilities and limitations of computers. MIS developed as a specialized field to bridge this gap, with shared knowledge from both the computing and business worlds.

An example of a business information system is an accounting system that records transactions and manages the accounting systems of an enterprise. Other examples are inventory management and tracking systems and point-of-sales systems (a cash register connected to an inventory system that automatically updates inventory with each purchase). Another example is a Web-based system to allow users to purchase items on the Web.

To be effective and efficient, each of these systems must be planned with defined goals and specific interactions between the employees and the computing systems.

The use of computers, the Internet, and the World Wide Web is a major area of focus in information systems. The application of this technology to business is an area called *e-commerce*, which covers everything from the business models involved to the technologies needed to handle transactions and order posting online.

16.2   BIOINFORMATICS

Bioinformatics is the application of computing, data mining, mathematics, and artificial intelligence to biological programs using high-performance computing machines. The research into DNA and genome sequencing and analysis of protein structures are areas of application that are yielding important results that will lead to improvements in health and quality of life.

Research into DNA and the genome sequencing will lead to an improved understanding of genetic disease, human growth, and lifespan. Analyzing protein structures can lead to predictions on the behavior of existing and potentially new proteins within a living organism.

Computers are also being used to simulate ecosystems to investigate changes and effects of populations, habitats, climate, and the like.

16.3   HEALTH CARE INFORMATICS

Health care informatics apply computer systems, data processing, and information systems ideas, techniques, and tools to the health care field. Application areas range widely and include:

- Automating the doctor's file on each patient, so that a doctor, physician's assistant, and nurse can all enter and retrieve information directly from a patient's chart. This saves time, reduces the risk of misplacing a file or losing important records, and can help ensure that critical patient information is not inadvertently overlooked when deciding on a course of treatment or medication regime.
- There are a variety of medical information systems currently in use, from images of a patient produced by a variety of devices, to patient charts, to hospital records, to drug effectiveness. Allowing the convenient exchange and integration of these different sources of data and different information systems is an area of study that focuses on the underlying structure of the data and building data formats and structures that support integration.
- Consolidated case histories and records of illness and treatment and drug regimes are important sources of information that can be mined for relationships. For instance, a pattern of illness present in a small minority of patients may otherwise be missed. If a disease pattern is so rare that a doctor is likely to encounter it only once every few years, the special circumstances are likely to be overlooked. However, through exploring data from many sources and physicians, underlying patterns and exceptions can be discovered, leading to targeted research and better treatment options.

16.4 GEOGRAPHICAL INFORMATION SYSTEMS

Geographical information systems (GIS) study the application of computing technology to managing and manipulating geographical data. A GIS is a system of hardware and software that stores geographical data and allows the user to analyze, display, and manage the data. A well-known application of GIS is to help determine locations and plot routes from place to place. Handheld navigation systems were pioneered by the military and are now common tools that can be commonly installed in cars.

GIS systems can be accessed in three primary ways:

1. **The database view:** A GIS is a database that contains geographical data. It can be accessed, managed, and searched like any database.
2. **Geovisualization:** A GIS provides a set of tools to translate the data into visual view. Maps can be created of the earth's surface that reveal the features and relationships of the underlying geology. Other information can also be overlaid on a map showing biosystem information (flora, fauna, ecology) and human activities (structures, roads, mining, drainage systems). This allows the GIS to aid in the creation of new knowledge by allowing the exploration of relationships between different information connected by geography. Geovisualization is used by cities and government agencies to display the locations of roads, utilities, property lines, drainage systems, easements, and the like.
3. **Geoprocessing:** A GIS contains a set of software tools that allow the transformation of existing data sets to create new data sets. These new data sets can reveal hidden relationships. Transformational functions are used to combine and transform existing data into a new set of dataset.

16.5 METEOROLOGY AND CLIMATOLOGY

Powerful computers are used to predict the movement and changes in weather patterns. This is based on the understanding of the physics of fluid dynamics and interactions between air masses of varying temperatures and barometric pressures. The more simulation points that can be included in the model, the better the overall predictions will be, so large computer systems and supercomputers are in use. The use of supercomputers for the earth simulator in Japan are powerful enough to model the earth as a system including atmosphere, ocean, vegetation, and man-made influences.

The use of computer modeling is central to the understanding and the predictions of global warming. Many scientists are working with alternative earth system models that simulate the globe differently and with different parameters and inputs. The majority of these models are predicting some level of global warming over the next few decades. This leads many to conclude that our understanding of the earth system is sufficiently advanced to allow reliable predictions, and that our ability to model the earth has attained sufficient accuracy as to lead to the further conclusion that the earth is currently in a warming trend. Some are sufficiently confident in these computer models to conclude that the global warming trend this is at least partly due to the production of CO^2 in the atmosphere as a byproduct of our use of technologies that require the consumption of fossil fuels.

16.6 COMPUTER GAMING

Computers have been used to build games since the first computer game (Space Travel) was developed in the 1960s by the lead developer of the UNIX operating system, which was the forerunner of the popular Linux operating system. Computer games are a multibillion dollar worldwide entertainment phenomena. Computer games can include aspects from many computing areas: digital graphics, computer animation, artificial intelligence, human–computer interaction, real-time operating systems, and multithreading, to name a few.

Computer games are related to computer simulations, in that both create an artificial world with rules that are in many ways similar to our real world. Obviously computer games include aspects that are more or less fantasy, while a simulation seeks to strictly model some aspect of reality in high fidelity.

Computer games have gone far beyond their commercial origins as video games. One of the first widely successful commercial video games was Pac-Man, by Namco. Pac-Man is an artificial world with rules and behaviors, no real artificial intelligence, and little logic and planning for players. Most of the player's ability is involved in hand–eye coordination and playing the game enough to learn the patterns, limitations, and opportunities.

Most computer games now require more human intelligence to play well, learn and devise strategies, and assess changing situations and scenarios. The higher level of intelligent interaction demanded of the human player implies that there is an artificial intelligence that the player is interacting with and essentially playing against. In the case of multiplayer games, the opposing intelligence is in the human opponents, and the computer logic is used to run the rules of the artificial world (which can be very complex and sophisticated).

Modern game development commonly requires a team of specialists under the direction of a game developer who has control of the "vision" of the design of the game. Computer programmers, graphic artists, designers, digital sound designers, and musicians collaborate to create and develop a game.

16.7   EMBEDDED SYSTEMS

Embedded systems is an area of applying computers by embedded computers in larger devices and systems. The term is also used to describe a field of study where the control and integration of small processors and computer systems are integrated as part of a larger system. Embedded systems are special-purpose systems where the computer is not available for general processing, but is dedicated to specific tasks within the overall larger system. Examples of embedded systems are numerous:

- The modern automobile has dozens of processors controlling a variety of functions, from braking to stability control to ignition timing, all interconnecting with sensors on a wired network within the vehicle itself.
- Digital televisions include processors to work with the media information and process it for display.
- Many common appliances include embedded processors to provide the control functions for the device and also to display information to the user (i.e., time, heat, intensity, and cycles).
- Modern buildings, smart homes, and home heating and cooling systems have gone digital, with computer chips linked to thermostats, sensors, and relays to sense the building's temperature and humidity and to control the various compressors and blowers.

Embedded systems in general must operate in *real time*, meaning that they must interact to inputs within real-timing constraints. For instance, an embedded computer in a building that takes 12 hours to respond to a drop in building temperature before turning on the heat would be considered a failure. Even though it responded to its inputs with the correct "output" response, it did not do so within a satisfactory time.

Building and designing embedded systems generally requires an understanding of the hardware-level functioning of the computer and other devices. The specifics about ports, timing, voltage levels, and sensor responses are all hardware-dependent engineering-type data that must be assimilated to build a successful embedded system.

The first embedded system was the inertial guidance system developed for the Apollo moon-landing spacecraft. Each Apollo spacecraft had one; both the command module and the lunar excursion module (LEM) had a guidance computer (see Figure 16.1).

FIGURE 16.1 Apollo Guidance Computer

CHAPTER 16 QUESTIONS

1. Think of another area where computers are applied or could be applied. Research on the Internet and write a paragraph explaining the application of computers and computing to this area.

2. List five devices in your home that contain computer chips.

3. List five toys that have computer chips embedded in them.

4. Research global warming computer models, which are also called climate change models. Describe these computer system models in a one-page report. List and reference your sources.

Computing and Societal Issues: Ethics, Global Computing, and Academic Integrity

This chapter is an introduction to societal issues involving computing, the science, the discipline, and personal responsibility. An overview of the outsourcing/global-sourcing phenomena is included. **Prerequisite knowledge needed:** Chapter 2.

17.0 Introduction

17.1 Ethical Issues

17.2 Global Computing and Outsourcing

17.3 Students and Ethics

17.0 INTRODUCTION

This chapter introduces the student to the idea that there are ethical implications to creating and developing computing systems, and that computer systems have an impact on human society and the economies of the world's nations. Also included is a section that describes a computing student's ethical obligation.

17.1 ETHICAL ISSUES

Computers are fully integrated into our daily lives and control functions and provide services that we depend on, from the mundane to the critical. A failure of a program or a chip in a personal computer is frustrating, but a failure of software or hardware on a critical system, such as in an aircraft, affects the lives of passengers. Levels of correctness and reliability are important—from the PC noncritical level to the life-threatening level. Software, hardware, and systems engineers and designers must create systems with a professional respect for the people who will use the systems.

Financial systems that handle money and personal records are associated with ethical issues from the obvious financial accuracy and theft aspect. Personal records are very important pieces of information that can be used in identity theft and sold as data to others who will use them in unauthorized ways.

Health systems contain the personal health records of individuals must be kept secure and private. The unauthorized access to these records can potentially damage the lives of people with health issues by denying employment, health insurance, and other effects.

Safety critical systems are those where human lives and welfare are dependent upon the proper functioning of the system and its hardware and software. Examples include aircraft and automobiles.

Voting systems are a relatively new application of modern computing technology, though the early punch-card devices where developed for the U.S. Census back in the late 1800s. These systems and all those who have access to their internal functioning must be vetted and approved. Tampering and security weaknesses in voting systems can misdirect elections and undermine voters' confidence in the outcomes.

It is incumbent on individuals working in the computing and information field to maintain the highest ethical standards in dealing with critical systems, financial systems, and systems containing personal data and records.

17.2 GLOBAL COMPUTING AND OUTSOURCING

The widespread use and adoption of the Internet has created a global economy where information can move anywhere in the world almost instantaneously and at extremely low cost. This has removed a barrier to the movement of jobs and industry that once needed to be close to the source of labor or the market for the goods and services for which the products are destined. Now, a worker whose product is information or the product can be represented in digital form can be located anywhere in the world and easily reach his or her customers and suppliers. Any job in design and engineering can potentially move anywhere on the globe, particularly including computer programming jobs. Jobs that need to be close to an organization or manufacturing machines are more resistant to this movement.

> **Outsourcing:** The reallocation of a job or set of tasks from an internal function (internal to an organization or company) to a contracted external function.
>
> **Offshoring:** The movement of jobs and manufacturing from within the home country of a firm to a manufacturer or supplier that is outside of the country—often to the Far East in countries such as India, China, Malaysia, and so forth.
>
> **Global Sourcing:** The phenomena or practice of moving jobs, tasks, and functions anywhere in the world, following the lowest cost of manufacturing or lowest labor cost, perhaps in multiple levels. For instance, a firm in the United States may outsource a function to a company that has an office in India. The office in India may do some of the work with Indian employees, but may choose to outsource part of the labor to China, following the lowest labor costs.

The computing professional needs to be aware of this highly significant way in which business is conducted in the modern global economy because it affects the employment market and career options in the computing fields. Computing technology is the enabling technology that makes the global economy possible. In building a career in computing, the professional needs to know that they are in a fast-changing field where basic technologies and fundamental truths about how to apply computing are subject to change.

Tasks and job function are not equally amenable to offshoring and global sourcing. It has been demonstrated that basic programming functions can be outsourced and global sourced relatively easily, with high productivity, to pursue the lowest cost of labor. These functions are characterized by well-defined and specified functions and task requirements that—when given to a competent and experience programmer—can be accomplished with a high degree of reliability with minimal confusion and miscommunication.

Conversely, tasks and jobs that cannot be easily outsourced or globally sourced are those that are poorly defined or are in a state of flux for which a fixed specification is not possible at any one time, and that require a high degree of interpersonal communication. Also, tasks and jobs that are critical to an organization and those that represent critical competitive advantages should not be outsourced.

Examples of functions that are not easily outsourced include:

- The high-level design of a new product or system whose specifications and goals are still in flux, in a marketplace with fluid competition and constant technological evolution.
- The design of a new technology that will provide an important competitive advantage when it is included in a new product. Internally developed proprietary technology innovation must be protected and secured and held closely within a company.
- The function of a chief executive officer or a chief financial officer generally cannot be outsourced, because that function is both integral to the organization and requires a very high degree of interactivity with other people.

Just as the Internet made the global economy flourish by removing cost barriers to the flow of information and digital products, technology enhancements will enhance the fluidity of the economy and facilitate remote collaborations. When people communicate, they interact in a rich medium that includes voice, facial expressions, gestures, body position, and body language. Distance collaboration and meetings over the network provides a limited subset of this rich medium; the voice is well represented and facial expressions are partially captured, while gestures and body language are only minimally communicated. The richness of the communication medium is related to cost in terms of communication bandwidth and high-quality live streaming video. As technology continues to improve and evolve, the ability to communicate fully through all human modes of expression will be enhanced, resulting in more effective distance communication through an experience that becomes closer and closer to the experience of a face-to-face meeting. This will result in wider application and an acceptance of distance communication, collaboration, and telecommuting in the future. This provides greater opportunities for personal satisfaction (the ability to live in a cabin in the mountains while running an engineering consulting firm), as well as increased global competition for work, which will tend to equalize wages worldwide.

17.3 STUDENTS AND ETHICS

It is incumbent on students that they apply themselves to their studies to maximize their effectiveness as a future employee and computing professional. The global economy and the evolution of distance collaboration tools will increase the competition for jobs and employment. Employees must seek to maximize the value they bring to an employer in order to support the firm in its quest to remain competitive and successful. A successful company will be able to provide high-quality employment opportunities. Companies that are struggling and are hit by the competition from overseas firms utilizing lower-cost professional labor are under great pressure to reduce their costs. The largest component of a firm's costs is usually the cost of its work-force.

Students must understand that ethical errors like cheating on exams, the unapproved collusion and collaboration on homework and projects, turning in another's program as one's own, and letting other team members carry the workload through group projects undermines the students' own knowledge and expertise. The student who engages in these activities damages his or her own ability to compete in the global marketplace and will damage their future employer's economic competitiveness through their marginal competence.

Students who graduate with marginal knowledge and competence will reflect poorly on their institution, damaging the reputation of the school. This in turn will affect the perceived value of their peers' diplomas. A student's opportunities after graduation are partly dependent on the perceived quality of the institution granting their degree. Students who cheat without detection will go on to graduate and accept a job where their level of competence and knowledge will be revealed, casting doubt on the quality of their institution and the capabilities of all graduates from their school. Cheating has unintended consequences that end up damaging fellow students, the institution, and the reputation of its professors. Naturally, it is then a responsibility of the professors and teachers to prohibit cheating and invest time in policies and procedures that prohibit, discourage, detect, and punish cheating in all forms. Students also share this responsibility to create a climate that discourages questionable ethical practices.

Students will go on to accept important jobs designing systems that other people will be dependent upon: safety critical systems where lives are at stake, financially critical systems where money is managed, and personal information systems where personal records of finance and health are stored and whose unauthorized access can damage individuals. Students in the computing field therefore must have the highest ethical standards.

Students must learn and respect the boundaries set by their professors:

- Professors often specify that no collaboration between students on any graded project or exam is allowed.

- Collaboration in the form of help on programming assignments may be allowed. If allowed, each student must ensure that they understand everything that is being shown to them and not allow a classmate or acquaintance to do a portion of the project for them.
- Students must respect the boundaries set for them on exams, and if allowed specific tools or resources during an exam, to restrict themselves to what is allowed.
- Plagiarism on papers and programs is never allowed. When including material from sources, those sources must be clearly referenced in one of the approved forms (and it is the student's responsibility to make themselves knowledgeable about what is an acceptable format). It is not acceptable to include material from sources and then when caught, claim that it was not copying or cheating but simply a failure to properly credit or reference the sources. A failure to reference sources is considered a form of copying and cheating.

CHAPTER 17 QUESTIONS

1. Using the internet as a research tool, write a paragraph for each area described below that describes and explains how some aspect of computing technology has improved:

   a. Business or Commerce

   b. Health care

   c. Scientific Research

   d. Education

2. This exploration has two aspects. Explore how technology can support collaboration at-a-distance with a partner(s) to explore the following question: Has the impact of computing technology always had positive effects?

   a. Answer the question with a one-page joint collaborative essay.

   b. Each member of the team will independently report on how distance collaboration enabled and hindered the collaboration effort. Each person should independently write a paragraph describing their observation of the experience.

   c. Exchange observations on the collaborative experience with your team member(s) and the rest of the class.

   d. Class exercise: List the positive and negative observations about distance collaboration and tally the number of participants reporting or observing each point. What observations (if any) were mentioned by half or more of the students in the class.

Computer Number Systems

A ppendix C is an introduction to basic computer number systems, number system conversions, and representation issues. **No prerequisite knowledge needed.**

A.1   DECIMAL SYSTEM: POWERS OF THE BASE

The decimal number system is based on powers of the base 10. The place value of each digit is a power of 10. We are so comfortable with the decimal number system that we don't even think about the underlying mechanisms. For instance, the number 1,259 uses digits in place values that are based on powers of the base (base 10):

```
the 9 is in the 10⁰ column — 1s column
the 5 is in the 10¹ column — 10s column
the 2 is in the 10² column — 100s column
the 1 is in the 10³ column — 1,000s column


1259 is

    9 X     1 = 9
  + 5 X    10 = 50
  + 2 X   100 = 200
  + 1 X 1,000 = 1,000
              - - - - -
              1,259
```

The computer's hardware logic is implemented with transistors, which can work like switches, turning electricity on or off. If we consider "on" to be a "1" and "off" to be "0," then internal computer logic can be represented using the binary number system. The binary number system uses the same mechanism as the decimal system just outlined, but the base is different— base 2 (binary) rather than base 10 (decimal). The place values for binary are based on powers of the base just as decimal is, but for binary the place values are powers of 2:

```
2⁷   2⁶   2⁵   2⁴   2³  2²  2¹  2⁰
128  64   32   16   8   4   2   1
```

Therefore, the binary number 10110011 can be converted to decimal so we can understand it, by using the powers-of-the-base mechanism:

```
1 0 1 1 0 0 1 1 =
                              1 X    1 = 1
                          1 X    2 = 2   |
                       0 X    4 = 0      |
                    0 X    8 = 0         |
                 1 X   16 = 16           |
              1 X   32 = 32              |
           0 X   64 = 0                  |
       1 X  128 = 128                    v
           |---------------------------| SUM
              = 179 in decimal
```

A.2 DIVISION/REMAINDER ALGORITHM: CONVERTING TO BINARY

Section A.1 explained how the decimal system works and how the binary system uses the same mechanism. In the process, a way to convert a binary number to a decimal number was revealed by using the powers-of-the-base system. To convert in the other direction, (from decimal to binary) requires a different method, which is called the *division/remainder method*. The idea is to repeatedly divide the decimal number to be converted by the base to be converted into (base 2). The remainders that result are the binary digits. For example, to convert 155 to binary you start from the bottom and work up.

```
                   Stop
              2)1    Q =  0, R = 1

              2)2    Q =  1, R = 0

              2)4    Q =  2, R = 0

              2)9    Q =  4, R = 1

              2)19   Q =  9, R = 1

              2)38   Q = 19, R = 0

              2)77   Q = 38, R = 1

Start:        2 )155 Q = 77, R = 1
```

The answer is 10011011. Be careful to read the digits in the correct order.

The answer can be checked with the powers-of-the-base system:

```
1 X    1 =    1
1 X    2 =    2
1 X    8 =    8
1 X   16 =   16
1 X  128 =  128
             - - - - -
             155
```

A.3   ADDITION IN BINARY

Just as in the decimal system, binary numbers can be added together. Because the base is different, the carryover to the next column is different. In the decimal system, when a column adds up to more than 9 a carry is added to the column to the left (which is the next higher place value). Because in the binary system the base is 2 (with digits of 0 and 1), when a sum evaluates to more than 1 then a carry must be added to the column to the left. Examples are:

```
    1
    1
+   1
   10


    1
  101
+   1
  110


111
 10110
+ 1101
100011
```

A.4   BITS, BYTES, AND WORDS

Bits are organized into groups inside the computer system. The most common grouping is to place eight bits in a byte. A byte just looks like a string of eight zeros and ones: 10101110. The range of possible binary values that a byte can hold is from 00000000 to 11111111.

TABLE A.1 Bits with Combinations

Number of bits	Number of combinations
1	$2^1 = 2$ combinations (0 and 1)
2	$2^2 = 4$ combinations, (00, 01, 10, 11)
6	$2^6 = 64$
10	$2^{10} = 1024$

There are 256 possible combinations of zeros and ones arranged in any order in a byte. The number of possible combinations is based on a power of the base:

$$2^{\#\text{of bits}} = \text{the number of combinations}$$

Examples are shown in Table A.1.

A byte can hold a small number or a single character. Characters are all the letters of the alphabet in upper and lower case, punctuation symbols, the digits 0–9, and can include other special symbols.

Bytes can be grouped together to form words. A word is simply one or more bytes, but it also has implications that relate to the computer's power. A computer with a word size of a single byte can work with and manipulate data 8 bits at a time (a rough approximation). A 16-bit computer (word size of two bytes) is more powerful, because it can access and manipulate 16 bits at a time rather than 8. Typical word sizes for common personal computers are 32 bit (4 bytes) and 64 bit (8 bytes).

Computer systems include large quantities of bytes; billions and trillions of bytes are becoming common. To deal with these large numbers, a type of shorthand was developed to refer to large numbers of bytes (see Table A.2).

TABLE A.2 Units of Bytes

Shorthand	Term	Roughly	Power of 2	Actual
K	Kilobyte	Thousand	2^{10}	1024
M or Meg	Megabyte	Million	2^{20}	1,048,576
G or Gig	Gigabyte	Billion	230	1,073,741,824
T	Terabyte	Trillion	240	1,099,511,627,776

A.5   HEXADECIMAL NUMBER SYSTEM

Another number system that is convenient to use in computing is the hexadecimal system. Hexadecimal is a base-16 number system. Just as the decimal system has a base of 10 (10 digits, 0–9) and binary is base 2 (2 digits, 0–1), the hexadecimal is base 16 (16 digits, 0–15).

However, representing the values from 10–15 is problematic; a single numeral is needed to represent those values. The solution is to use the first six letters of the alphabet for the integers from 10 to 15:

```
0  1  2  3  4  5  6  7  8  9   A   B   C   D   E   F
0  1  2  3  4  5  6  7  8  9  10  11  12  13  14  15
```

Note that just as the decimal system includes digits for 0–9 and the 10 is two digits (with the "1" in the "tens" column), the hexadecimal system includes digits for 0–15 and 16 is represented with a "1" in the "sixteens" column. In the hexadecimal system, "10" is worth 16 in decimal.

The same place-value mechanism that is used in decimal and binary also is applied to hexadecimal, where place values are based on powers of the base, which in this case is base 16. For example, the hexadecimal number 1B52 can be converted to our more familiar decimal system using the same powers of the base mechanism used in previous conversions:

```
the 2 is in the 16⁰ column — 1s column
the 5 is in the 16¹ column — 16s column
the B (11) is in the 16² column — 256s column
the 1 is in the 16³ column — 4096s column
```

$1B52_{16}$ is

```
      2 X     1 =     2
  +  5 X    16 =    80
  + 11 X   256 =  2816
  +  1 X  4096 =  4096
                -----
              6994₁₀
```

Subscripts are often used to indicate the base of the number, which is not always apparent just from looking at the digits.

Hexadecimal turns out to be a useful and convenient number system for working with binary digital computers because of the relationship between base 16 and base 2. Sixteen is a convenient power of the base 2: $2^4 = 16$. Four binary (base 2) digits that span values from 0000–1111 (0–15) cover the exact same set of value as one hexadecimal digit (0–15). Thus, a group of four bits can be conveniently represented as a single hexadecimal digit. This is illustrated as follows:

Base 2, Binary	Base 16, Hexadecimal
0000	0
0001	1
0010	2
0011	3
0100	4
0101	5
0110	6
0111	7
1000	8
1001	9
1010	A
1011	B
1100	C
1101	D
1110	E
1111	F

Therefore, if a group of four binary digits can be represented with a single hexadecimal digit, then an 8-bit byte can be conveniently represented with just two hexadecimal digits:

Binary	Hexadecimal
0001 0001	11
1000 1000	88
1100 1011	CB
1111 0111	F7

Note that it is far more convenient to talk about digital binary values in hexadecimal than it is in binary. For instance, a 16-bit binary value: "1100100100100101" (difficulty to say and hear) can be easily shared or recorded as "C925."

Converting from binary to hexadecimal (often abbreviated as just *hex*) and hex to binary is easily done without a formal conversion process, simply by grouping bits into groups of four, and translating that binary value to its equivalent hex digit. At first the student may need to use decimal as an intermediary:

1001	→	9	→	9
1101	→	13	→	D

F	→	*15*	→	*1111*
7	→	*7*	→	*0111*

Converting multidigit values:

Binary							**Hex**
01101001	→	0110 1001	→	6,9	→		69
10110001	→	1011 0001	→	11,1	→		B1

Hex						**Binary**
A8	→	10,8	→	1010 1000	→	10101000
3F	→	3,15	→	0011 1111	→	00111111

A.6   NEGATIVE NUMBERS

So far we have worked with unsigned binary values, but number systems need to be able to represent both positive and negative numbers. For the purposes of this discussion, we will limit ourselves to values with eight binary bits.

In eight bits, a range of values can be represented. There are 256 possible combinations of 0s and 1s with eight bits, ranging from 00000000 to 11111111. An examination of the range of values follows:

Binary	**Hex**	**Decimal**
00000000	00	0
00000001	01	1
00000010	02	2
00000011	03	3
.	.	.
.	.	.
.	.	.
11111100	FC	252
11111101	FD	253
11111110	FE	254
11111111	FF	255

With eight bits (one byte) there are 256 possible combinations allowing values from 0 to 255. The number of combinations is also based on the powers of the base mechanisms because $2^8 = 256$.

However, in order to represent negative numbers (in eight bits), some of the available values must be dedicated to represent negative numbers, and some to positive numbers. The obvious first idea is to use a method called sign-magnitude representation.

Sign-Magnitude Representation

The most obvious way to include representations for negative numbers is to use one of the binary digits as a sign bit rather than a number value. The sign bit indicates whether the number is to be positive or negative. The convention is to use the left-most bit for the sign bit, and to use zero to mean that the number is positive number and to use a one when the number is negative. The available combinations of 0s and 1s now have a different meaning:

Binary	Hex	Decimal
S		
00000000	00	+0 positive (?) zero
00000001	01	+1
00000010	02	+2
00000011	03	+3
.	.	.
.	.	.
.	.	.
01111110	7E	+126
01111111	7F	+127
10000000	80	-0 negative (?) zero
10000001	81	-1
10000010	82	-2
.	.	.
.	.	.
.	.	.
11111100	FC	-124
11111101	FD	-125
11111110	FE	-126
11111111	FF	-127

Two problems with sign-magnitude representation are apparent from this table of values:

1. There are two representations for zero, both a positive zero and a negative zero.
2. Two representations for zero waste one of the combinations that could otherwise be used more productively.

A third problem with sign-magnitude representation is revealed only when attempting basic mathematics. For instance, adding a positive and negative number should work correctly, but does not using sign-magnitude representation:

```
        7         00000111
 +    −5         10000011
  -----          -------
        2         10001010   = −12!
```

The problem with working with positive and negative numbers can be fixed for sign magnitude internally inside the computer chip. Addition circuits can be designed to work correctly for adding numbers of each combination of signs of values:

```
    +    +    −    −
    +    −    +    −
```

Four different addition circuits can be designed inside the CPU to handle each case, but this requires four times the circuitry and transistors to implement, which is clearly not efficient. In addition, there are special cases that need be handled for other operations, not just addition. Each case also must correctly recognize the two different representations for zero. These problems lead to the solution, which is called two's complement representation.

Two's Complement

A better approach than sign-magnitude is a method called two's complement. It is more complicated and is not intuitive, and only the unsolvable problems of the sign-magnitude representation force the use of two's complement representation. Still, two's complement does indeed work correctly and avoids the need for separate circuits to implement math with combinations of positive and negative numbers.

As with sign-magnitude, in two's complement representation a single bit is used to represent the sign of the number, and it is the left-most bit that is used for the sign, but the meaning of the combinations of bits is different than in sign magnitude representation for the negative numbers. The negative numbers count down from −128 in the progression-of-bit combinations:

Binary	Hex	Decimal
S		
00000000	00	+0
00000001	01	+1
00000010	02	+2
00000011	03	+3
.	.	.
.	.	.
.	.	.
01111110	7E	+126
01111111	7F	+127
10000000	80	-128
10000001	81	-127
10000010	82	-126
.	.	.
.	.	.
.	.	.
11111100	FC	-4
11111101	FD	-3
11111110	FE	-2
11111111	FF	-1

It is now difficult to "read" a negative number, because the meaning of the bits are reversed (complemented) from the more familiar binary. And note that there is now only one representation for zero, and that this extra combination made available allows an extra value to be represented, which is used for -128. Therefore, the combinations with the zero as the sign bit range from 0 to 127, and the combinations with the one as the sign bit range from -128 down to -1.

Fortunately, there is a simple way to "translate" or understand the meanings of the negative values, and it is how this representation system got its name. To convert a positive value to its negative representation in two's complement, a two-step process is used:

Start with the binary positive representation:

1. Complement (reverse) all the bits (one's complement).
2. Add one (making it two's complement).

Example: Find the two's-complement representation of -3:

```
A positive 3 in eight-bits is:    00000011
Complementing the bits:            11111100
Add one:                          +00000001
                                   ---------
                                   11111101 = -3
```

Observe that this is the same value for -3 shown in the previous table of values.

The same two's complement steps can also be used to translate or convert a negative value:

```
A 23 in 8-bits is:        11111101
Complementing the bits:   00000010
Add one:                 +00000001
                          ---------
                          00000011 = +3
```

Therefore, a negative two's complement value can be "read" by finding its positive value equivalent for the magnitude of the number, and remembering that it's the negative of that value.

Two's Complement and Math

Two's complement does solve the problem with working with combinations of positive- and negative-signed numbers:

```
      7              00000111  = +7
+   -5              11111011  = -5
-----               --------
      2            1 00000010  = +2!
```

Notice that the carry from the addition of ones to the next place value carries over beyond the eight bits. Inside the computer, this result is noted but the bit is discarded (slightly amusingly described as thrown into the "bit bucket," though there is no actual "bit bucket" inside the machine).

Another example:

```
     -7             11111001  = -7
+    -5             11111011  = -5
-----               --------
    -12            1 11110100  = -12!
```

APPENDIX A EXERCISES

Work out the following problems on paper (show your work). Convert from binary to decimal:

1. 1001
2. 0011
3. 10011000
4. 01001101

Work the following problems, converting decimal to binary (show your work).

5. 7
6. 15
7. 113
8. 238

Work the following programs, representing the following decimal numbers in two's complement binary in eight bits.

9. 12
10. 100
11. −30
12. −97

Boolean Algebra

This appendix is an introduction to Boolean algebra, useful for understanding the logic foundations of binary computer systems. The section introduces the basic terminology of Boolean algebra and the representation of functions in truth table. **Prerequisite knowledge needed:** Chapter 4.

B.1 INTRODUCTION TO BOOLEAN ALGEBRA

Boolean algebra was developed in the 1840s by mathematician George Boole. In Boolean algebra, there are two elements:

```
0   false or OFF
1   true or ON
```

There are three operations:

OR using the addition operator: +
AND using the multiplication operator or a dot: ·
NOT (reverse or complement) using a horizontal line over the term or value: ⎯

The following are simple truisms or identities:

```
0 + 0 = 0
0 + 1 = 1 + 0 = 1
1 + 1 = 1

0 · 0 = 0
0 · 1 = 1 · 0 = 0
1 · 1 = 1
```

A Boolean variable is represented with capital letters and can take on the value 0 or 1.

Boolean function maps input values to output values. Only Boolean variables, elements, and operations are allowed in a Boolean function. For example,

```
ƒ(A,B) = A + B
```

Possible combinations of values for Boolean variables A and B are:

```
ƒ(A,B) = A + B
ƒ(0,0) = 0 + 0 = 0
ƒ(0,1) = 0 + 1 = 1
ƒ(1,0) = 1 + 0 = 1
ƒ(1,1) = 1 = 1 = 1
```

Because each variable can assume only two values, the number of possible combinations of values is $2^{\#variables}$. A truth table can be created that represents the same information as just noted:

A	B	A + B
0	0	0
0	1	1
1	0	1
1	1	1

B.2   PERFECT INDUCTION

Perfect induction is a proof technique that lists every possible combination or case in order to prove the truth or falseness of the hypothesis. Perfect induction is doable only in cases where the number of cases or combinations is finite, because every case must be listed. For Boolean problems, the number of cases is finite and often of manageable size based on $2^{\#variables}$.

As an example, a truth table will be used to prove the equivalency of two Boolean functions using perfect induction:

$$f(A,B) = A + AB$$

$$g(A,B) = A(A + B)$$

A	B	AB	f = A + AB	A + B	g = A(A + B)
0	0	0	**0**	0	**0**
0	1	0	**0**	1	**0**
1	0	0	**1**	1	**1**
1	1	1	**1**	1	**1**

By comparing all values for f and g, the equivalence of the two functions is proven. A second example investigates the truth value of

$$(A + B)(A + C) \ ?= \ A + BC$$

Note that here there are three Boolean variables present, and hence eight combinations of values that must be examined.

A	B	C	A + B	A + C	(A + B)(A + C)	BC	A + BC
0	0	0	0	0	**0**	0	**0**
0	0	1	0	1	**0**	0	**0**
0	1	0	1	0	**0**	0	**0**
0	1	1	1	1	**1**	1	**1**
1	0	0	1	1	**1**	0	**1**
1	0	1	1	1	**1**	0	**1**
1	1	0	1	1	**1**	0	**1**
1	1	1	1	1	**1**	1	**1**

By comparing all possible values for the two terms their equivalence is proven.

B.3   DEMORGAN'S THEOREM

DeMorgan's theorem is very useful for building digital circuits because it provides a way to convert from AND gates to NOR gates and from OR gates to NAND gates. NAND and NOR gates have manufacturing and implementation advantages over the use of AND and OR gates.

DeMorgan's theorem states: "The complement of a product is the sum of the complements"—or stated in Boolean terms:

Th.1 "The complement of an AND is an OR of the complements."

and

Th.2 "The complement of an OR is the AND of the complements."

which can be remembered as:

"Distribute the complement and reverse the operation between the terms."

Perfect induction through a truth table will be used to prove the validity of DeMorgan's theorem:

Th.1	A	B	AB	$\overline{AB}$	$\overline{A}$	$\overline{B}$	$\overline{A} + \overline{B}$
	0	0	0	1	1	1	**1**
	0	1	0	1	1	0	**1**
	1	0	0	1	0	1	**1**
	1	1	1	**0**	0	0	**0**

Th.2	A	B	A + B	$\overline{A + B}$	$\overline{A}$	$\overline{B}$	$\overline{AB}$
	0	0	0	1	1	1	**1**
	0	1	1	**0**	1	0	**0**
	1	0	1	**0**	0	1	**0**
	1	1	1	**0**	0	0	**0**

B.4   DISTRIBUTIVE PROPERTY

The distributive property holds for Boolean algebra. This is demonstrated using perfect induction:

$$A(B + C) \ ? = AB + AC$$

A	B	C	B + C	A(B + C)	AB	AC	AB + AC
0	0	0	0	0	0	0	0
0	0	1	1	0	0	0	0
0	1	0	1	0	0	0	0
0	1	1	1	0	0	0	0
1	0	0	0	0	0	0	0
1	0	1	1	1	0	1	1
1	1	0	1	1	1	0	1
1	1	1	1	1	1	1	1

$$A + BC \ ? = \ (A + B)(A + C)$$

A	B	C	BC	A + BC	A + B	A + C	(A + B)(A + C)
0	0	0	0	0	0	0	0
0	0	1	0	0	0	1	0
0	1	0	0	0	1	0	0
0	1	1	1	1	1	1	1
1	0	0	0	1	1	1	1
1	0	1	0	1	1	1	1
1	1	0	0	1	1	1	1
1	1	1	1	1	1	1	1

B.5   DUALITY

The duality property of Boolean expressions states that for a given Boolean expression: Exchanging the operators (AND → OR, OR → AND), and exchanging any 0s and 1s (0 → 1, 1 → 0) will result in a different Boolean expression, which is also true.

Two simple examples:

$A + 1 = 1$	*its dual is*	$A \cdot 0 = 0$
$A \cdot 1 = A$	*its dual is*	$A + 0 = A$

For a more complex example, consider this expression:

$$A(B + C) = AB + AC$$

Its dual is:

$$A + BC = (A + B)(A + C)$$

The truth value of both of these expressions (which are duals of each other) is previously proven by perfect induction in Section B.4 when demonstrating the distributed property.

B.6   ADDITIONAL BOOLEAN ALGEBRA PROPERTIES

The **commutative law** holds for Boolean expressions.

$$AB = BA$$

$$A + B = B + A$$

Note that these expressions are duals of each other.

The **associative law** holds for Boolean expressions.

$$A(BC) = (AB)C$$

$$A + (B + C) = (A + B) + C$$

Note that these expressions are duals of each other. A proof by perfect induction that $A(BC) = (AB)C$ is:

A	B	C	BC	**A(BC)**	AB	**(AB)C**
0	0	0	0	**0**	0	**0**
0	0	1	0	**0**	0	**0**
0	1	0	0	**0**	0	**0**
0	1	1	1	**0**	0	**0**
1	0	0	0	**0**	0	**0**
1	0	1	0	**0**	0	**0**
1	1	0	0	**0**	1	**0**
1	1	1	1	**1**	1	**1**

Because the second associative example is a dual of the first, it is also true.

DeMorgan's theorem generalized:

$$\overline{ABC...n} = \overline{A} + \overline{B} + \overline{C}...+ \overline{n}$$

$$\overline{A + B + C...+ n} = \overline{A}\,\overline{B}\,\overline{C}...\overline{n}$$

Double complements and cancellation:

$$\overline{\overline{A}} = A$$

Absorption:

$$A + AB = A$$

And its dual:

$$A(A + B) = A$$

Absorption is proven by perfect induction:

A	B	AB	A + AB	A + B	A(A + B)
0	0	0	0	0	0
0	1	0	0	1	0
1	0	0	1	1	1
1	1	1	1	1	1

APPENDIX B EXERCISES

1. Prove by perfect induction that $A + (B + C) = (A + B) + C$

2. Prove by perfect induction whether $f = g$. $f(A,B) = A + BC$, $g(A,B) = A(B + C)$

3. Simplify the following expressions using Boolean algebra properties.
   a. $A + B(B + C)$
   b. $A(A + C) + AB + AC$
   c. $(A + B) + (A + BC)$

Gates and Simple Devices

T his appendix introduces the construction and hardware implementation of simple logic devices using discrete gates. Complexity is built up step-by-step, with an informal treatment, leading to simple devices and a simple memory device. **Prerequisite knowledge needed:** Appendix B.

C.1   SELECTOR

The first device to be considered is a selector (Figure C.1). This device is of limited use by itself but is a building block for other more sophisticated constructions. The selector allows the selection of one of two inputs, using a single control line.

In this figure, the control line is labeled Clk for Clock. When the clock is high (1), only the input at A produces an output that can vary. The value at B does not matter, because the results of the AND at B is guaranteed to be low (0) by the complement of the Clk (which is 0 when Clk is 1). When the clock is low (0), the input at A is irrelevant; only B can affect the output of its AND gate. The Clk control line determines which input, A or B, can have any affect on the outputs. This building block will be utilized in the following devices.

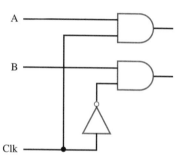

FIGURE C.1   Selector

C.2   TWO-TO-ONE MULTIPLEXOR

The next device uses the selector to build a multiplexor (Figure C.2). The *multiplexor* is a device that allows multiple inputs to take turns sharing one output. In this example, two inputs are combined into one shared output line. The value of the Clk control line determines which input (A or B) flows through to the output.

When the Clk is high (1), the value at input A flows through the AND gate and determines the value of the output after the OR. The value at B is irrelevant because the inverted Clk forces the value at its AND to a zero. Therefore, the output of the OR will only be 1 if the input at A is 1.

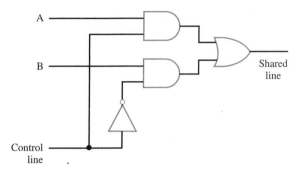

FIGURE C.2   Multiplexor

C.3   ONE-TO-TWO DEMULTIPLEXOR

The *demultiplexor* (Figure C.3) does the opposite of a multiplexor; it takes a single input and sends it to one of two outputs, depending on the value of a control line. This device is very similar to the selector, but with the inputs wired together.

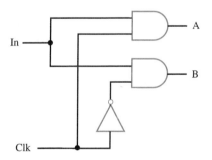

FIGURE C.3   Demultiplexor

C.4   MULTIPLEXOR/DEMULTIPLEXOR PAIR

The multiplexor and demultiplexor are used together to allow sharing a communication line. When the devices are tied together with a common clock, they allow multiple lines to share a common data line. Figure C.4 shows two input lines sharing a single common data line, but the concept can be expanded to many inputs, all taking turns using a common data line.

The multiplexor/demultiplexor pair is a classic data communications device, allowing shared access over both short and long distances. If the cost

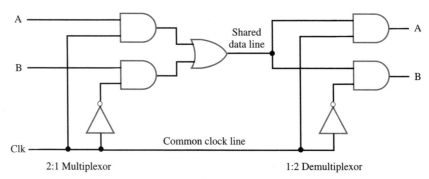

FIGURE C.4   Multiplexor System

of the shared line is high, because it must go long distances or perhaps because the short distances is a part of a many bit/line bus, a multiplexor/demultiplexor pair can reduce overall cost of the communication link.

If the multiplexor/demultiplexor pair is controlled by a single clock line (as in Figure C.4), it is using time division multiplexing (TDM), where access to the shared line rotates over time, depending on the values of the clock line.

C.5   SIMPLE MEMORY DEVICE

The simple two-to-one multiplexor of Figure C.2 can be used as the foundation for a simple memory device. A memory device should retain its current value, which can be read and also allow new values to be stored or written to it. A single control line can be used to select between these two functions (Read/Write).

In Figure C.5 the heavy blue line shows the feedback that is a crucial component of memory devices. The feedback line allows the current output

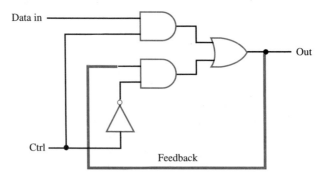

FIGURE C.5   Simple Memory Device

to flow back in as an input in order for the device to maintain its currently stored value. When the control line is 0 (READ), the output flows back around through the AND gate and back into the OR gate. The current output, regardless of whether it is a 0 or a 1, determines the future output.

In order to store (WRITE) a new value into the device, the value to be written must be present on the input, and then the Ctrl line is set to 1 (WRITE). In this state, the input flows through its AND gate to determine the value of the OR gate. If the input is a 1, the output becomes a 1. If the input is a 0, the output becomes a 0.

C.6 ADDITION CIRCUIT

A simple circuit with only four gates can implement the addition of two bits—a core operation required of a computer. This is implemented in a device call a half-adder (called this because two are needed to handle the case when there is a carry from a lower bit addition). A truth table that explains the function of the half-adder follows:

The device has two input bits, labeled A and B. Those two bits are added together to produce a SUM. The SUM consists of two bits, S_0 for the "ones column" and S_1 for the "twos column" when two 1s add together to make a 2.

Note that the production of the "ones column" (S_0) looks like an OR operation, producing a 1 for the output if either of the inputs is a 1, except when *both* inputs are a 1. This operation is known as an exclusive OR operation. The production of the twos column (S_1) looks like an AND—producing a 1 only when *both* inputs are a 1. These observations are the key to building the half-adder shown in Figure C.6.

Note that in Figure C.6, the half-adder ORs the two inputs to produce the low-order bit (S_0) and uses an AND to produce the high-order bit (S_1). The invertor and AND are used together to produce the correct low-order

TABLE C.I   Half-Adder Truth Table

		Sum
A	**B**	$S_1 S_0$
0	0	0 0
0	1	0 1
1	0	0 1
1	1	1 0

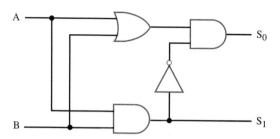

FIGURE C.6   Addition of Two Bits

bit (S_0), in the case when *both* inputs are 1. In that case, the output of the OR must be turned off.

Index

Italicized page locators indicate a figure/photo; tables are noted with a *t*.

Photograph Credits

Chapter 1

p. 7: Computer History Museum, Mountain View, CA. Courtesy of the Computer History Museum, Mountain View, CA.

p. 20: IBM5150. © IBM Corporate Archives.

p. 21: Dial on Computer Developed by Charles Babbage. © Photos.com.

p. 24: Atanasoff-Berry Computer Replica at Iowa State University. Courtesy of Iowa State University Library/Special Collections Department.

p. 25: IBM Mark I Computer. © IBM Corporate Archives.

Chapter 2

p. 32: Portrait of Von Neumann. Courtesy of Los Alamos National Laboratory.

Chapter 3

p. 52: Portrait of Ada Lovelace. © Queen's Printer and Controller of HMSO. UK Government Art Collection.

Chapter 4

p. 82: Portrait of Augustus De Morgan. © The College Collection Photos, UCL Library Services, Special Collections.

Chapter 16

p. 215: Apollo Display and Keyboard Unit. Courtesy of Dryden Flight Research Center/NASA.